tHe'S'word

JAMES ROY worked for many years as a paediatric and emergency nurse in various hospitals. He also spent five years working in the adolescent unit of the Children's Hospital at Westmead, in Sydney. In addition to his work with young people in the health setting, he has written several award-winning books for children and adolescents. James lives in a slightly creaky house with his wife, two daughters, and two Jack Russell terriers, one of whom has a brain the approximate size of a peanut. *The 'S' Word* is James's first work of non-fiction.

GUS GORDON decided after leaving school that 'drawing silly pictures' was a sensible career option, given his childhood obsession with drawing. He has illustrated over 40 children's books (that's a lot of pictures!) When Gus isn't drawing, he's usually chasing his two boys around their house. He also enjoys painting, listening to weird music, eating ham, cheese and avocado sandwiches — sometimes all at the same time!

the 'S' word

JAMES ROY

ILLUSTRATED BY GUS GORDON

THE O'BRIEN PRESS
DUBLIN

This edition first published 2008 by The O'Brien Press Ltd.
12 Terenure Road East, Rathgar, Dublin 6, Ireland.
Tel: +353 1 4923333; Fax: +353 1 4922777
E-mail: books@obrien.ie
Website: www.obrien.ie
Originally published 2006 by University of Queensland Press, Brisbane,
Australia

ISBN: 978-1-84717-056-9

British Library Cataloguing-in-Publication Data
Roy, James
The 'S' Word
1. Puberty - Juvenile literature 2. Sex instruction for teenagers - Juvenile literature
3. Adolescence - Juvenile literature 4. Teenagers - Life skills guides - Juvenile
literature
I. Title
612.6'61'08351

1 2 3 4 5 6 7 8 9 10
08 09 10 11 12 13 14

Printed by Leo Paper Products Ltd, China

dEDICATION

For Lachlan, Bailey, Zac and all the young men
who are wondering if anyone else has ever
done this before.
– J.R.

To my parents, for somehow getting four boys
through puberty — just!
– G.G.

contents

1   SeX AND FOOTBALL

On a cold night a few years ago I was at a football match. The stadium was almost completely full and it felt great to be there. The air was thick with the smells of chips and hotdogs, and supporters were proudly wearing their teams' colours. People were shouting, cheering and waving their banners as the teams ran out onto the field. It really was an amazing place to be.

But do you know what was going through my head as I gazed around that huge grandstand? I was actually thinking, *That's a lot of sex.* Because as I looked at those sixty thousand spectators, it suddenly dawned on me that every one of them was there because at some time, somewhere, their parents had had sex. And yes, that is *heaps* of sex. Don't try too hard to imagine sixty thousand couples 'doing it' — you might hurt your brain. But it definitely happened.

Maybe I'm a bit weird, thinking something like that at a football game. But I do know this: boys and men think about sex *a lot*.

A few years ago no one talked much to kids about sex. Ask your grandparents how much they were told when they were young, and they'll probably say 'Not much'. Sex wasn't discussed very often, and this doesn't seem right to me, when you consider that sex is a completely natural part of being a person, just as natural as eating, sleeping and going to the toilet. And just like any-thing else to do with you and who you are, it's nice to know what's going on. After all, you're probably going to have sex one day. As well as that, the things that happen to your body when you're changing from a boy into a man can be a bit confusing and sometimes even a little frightening. But there's really no need for them to be confusing *or* frightening, once you know what's going on.

So that's what this book is about. It's about you and your body, and sex. And when I say sex, I don't just mean the 'doing it' part. No, I mean everything to do with the way your body changes as you become an adult, the kinds of relationships you have, what you think about issues like being gay, or when you think you're old enough to have sexual intercourse. Because sex does also mean 'having sex', or 'doing it' with someone. Intercourse is often the bit that people think of first when they hear the word *sex*, but really it's about a lot more than just that.

This book is written for boys, so of course there's going to be some stuff in here about girls. But the females of the species aren't always easy to understand, so later in the book you'll find some tips for dealing with those strange, mysterious, frustrating but wonderful creatures called girls.

Even though this book is meant for boys rather than adult men, don't be surprised if you find your dad or even your grandad flipping through it, or even reading it

Doctor, is there any way I can stop thinking about sex?

Yes, but we would need to remove your brain.

closely. The truth is that males never stop thinking about sex, no matter how old they are.

As you read on, you're going to find out about some things that you might think are a bit gross, and other stuff that will make you feel strangely excited. In other words, all this sex talk will create emotions and feelings. That's because the biggest sex organ you have is your brain. Yes, your brain. And the best thing for your brain is to exercise it with information, which is what this book is chock full of.

tHE BIGGEST SeX ORGAN YOU HAVE IS YOUR BRAIN

Throughout the book a good friend of mine, Richard the Wise, will be answering some of the letters and emails he's received from boys and young men like you. These young men have written to him about some of their problems, concerns and questions, and Richard has tried to answer them honestly and directly. He can be a bit tough and direct at times, but that's only because he cares. Or so he tells me.

Finally, there might be a few adults who have a problem with you reading a book like *The 'S' Word*. They might think that you're too young, or that you don't need to know these things. They might even believe that reading this information is going to make you think dirty thoughts and go out there trying to have sex all the time. I'm quite certain this won't happen, and it's definitely not why the book was written. You're holding this book because, as a growing young man, you deserve to know about this very important part of your life.

So let's start with a look at what sex actually is.

From: BigBoy

To: richard_the_wise@hotmail.com

Subject: Mum doesn't understand

My mum thinks that I'm going to be a fashion designer, because every time she comes into my room she finds me reading about sewing machines in the encyclopaedia. What she doesn't know is that *Sewing Machine* is the topic just before *Sex*, and I've just flipped back a page so I don't get busted. I don't want her to think that I'm gay, but I don't want to get embarrassed either.

BigBoy

From: richard_the_wise@hotmail.com

To: BigBoy

Subject: Re: Mum doesn't understand

OK, two things, right off the top. First, even if you were going to be a fashion designer, it wouldn't make you gay. It might make you boring, but not gay. Plus, there are worse things in the world than being gay.

Second, I reckon your mum already knows the real reason for your apparent interest in sewing machines and is just having a bit of a joke with you. Why do I think that? Because your mum's not as stupid as you think she is. And also (don't be shocked), she used to be a kid once.

There are a couple of things you can do. You can just say to your mum, 'Mum, I'm trying to find out about sex.' Or you can say nothing and let her think what she likes. Or, as a final resort, you could try locking your bedroom door. She might think you're in there playing with yourself, but since she knows everything anyway, she already knows you're doing that.

So chill out, read up on sex, sewing machines or whatever else takes your fancy, and if you *are* in fact thinking of a career in fashion, you might want to start saying 'Fabulous!' and 'Darling!' a lot more, and wearing sunglasses around the house, even at night. If nothing else, it will soften the blow for your parents later on.

Happy sewing,

RICHARD THE WISE

2 WHAT IS SeX?

You might think that you already know what sex is. And maybe you do. Maybe you've asked your parents where babies come from, and they've told you how a man's sperm joins with a woman's egg to form a new baby. You might even know exactly what goes where when two people 'have sex'. But if that's all you know, then you're missing half of the picture, maybe even more.

Are you still there?

Yeah- I'm wiggling like crazy - what are you doing?

You see, sex isn't just two people taking off their clothes and wiggling about. It's way more than that. Sex helps make you the person you are, for a start. One of the first things people ask when a baby is born is, 'Is it a boy or a girl?' Of course, most parents don't mind whether they have a son or a daughter, as long as their baby is healthy. But which one you are — a boy or a girl — affects the kinds of friends you have, the way people look at you, the way you might be expected to behave, what you're interested in, and even the kinds of subjects you study at school. Boys are often told that they shouldn't cry, that they should 'be a man', big and strong and tough. And girls might be expected to play with particular kinds of toys, or be interested in certain types of movies, or to only play 'girls' sports', like netball.

Then, as you get older, being a man or a woman might affect the kind of job or career you think you should have. This happens much less than it used to, but it's still tough for a woman who wants to be a builder, for example, or for a guy who wants to get a job as a child-care worker. This is because people have learned to think of some jobs as men's work and others as women's work, and sometimes it takes a while to change people's ideas.

So sex helps make you who you are. But sex also means a whole bunch of other stuff as well. The way your body changes as you get older and become an adult is part of sex too. Waking up with an erection, or having sexy dreams at night, or playing with your penis in the shower, is part of you learning about sex. So is borrowing an art book from the library so you can look at nude paintings, or reading certain magazines, or surfing the Internet for pictures of naked people.

Check it out! Under those clothes she is TOTALLY naked!

FASHION STUFF

When you suddenly stop running away from girls because of their germs, and start watching them instead, and feel like you want to be near them and impress them, that's sex. It might not seem like it, but it is. And that urge you get to touch or kiss a girl you really like, or the fact that you think some girls are nicer than others, is also a part of sex. Or you might even find boys more attractive than girls, and learning that you're gay is part of sex as well.

And of course that leads us to the whole relationship thing. How you begin a relationship with someone special, how you keep it going and how you show that person the way you feel about them is a huge part of the topic. And it can be quite complicated, even knowing the difference between liking someone, loving someone, or simply having a huge crush on someone.

Sex is also physical, which I'm sure you already knew. Kissing, hugging, holding hands, touching each other, just sitting side by side on the beach with someone you really like is part of sex. That's right, you don't have to take your clothes off for it to be sex! But what most people think of when they hear the word 'sex' is intercourse — actually 'doing it' or 'having sex'. In the ratings that censors give to films and television shows, they talk about *sex scenes*, but they're not talking about a couple hugging or kissing or having a relationship. They almost always mean intercourse, which might be why it can all get a bit confusing.

YOU DON'T HAVE TO TAKE YOUR CLOTHES OFF FOR IT TO BE SeX!

In a lot of ways intercourse is the most exciting part of sex, maybe because it's the most private thing you can do with someone you really like. Plus it feels good. The other reason humans find it so exciting is because way down inside we want to create new humans, and of course sexual intercourse is how we reproduce, or make babies. It's not that different from other animals, who can't help trying to make new, baby versions of themselves. So as you can see, the desire to have sex is totally natural, and can be very hard to resist.

One of the most important parts of learning about sex is knowing the right way to behave. Because sex and relationships and love are so complex, it can sometimes be hard to know what to say and do when it comes to all this stuff.

But what makes it so complicated, really? For a start, sex and love feel good. Really good. We all want to be loved. Wanting to be loved is one of the most powerful forces there is. But, unfortunately, sometimes we get love and sex mixed up, and think that we have to have sex to show someone that we love them, or that we have to have sex to feel loved in the first place. But really, that's all back to front. Sex should be something that happens because two people love each other and because they *both* want to show it, not because one person thinks that they owe it to the other. Intercourse because you feel you have to do it is sex, but it's not love. See the difference?

SEX AND LOVE FEEL GOOD. reaLLY GOOD

One of the most important things for a young person to understand is that it's OK to *not* have sex. These days a lot of young people are having sex too early. Their bodies are ready, but the rest of them isn't. Once you finally get that close to someone, life can start to get even more complicated, especially if you suddenly find out that your girlfriend and you are about to become Mummy and Daddy. But even if that difficult situation doesn't happen, sex can really change who you are, not always in good ways.

Plus you might have friends pressuring you to 'lose your virginity' (which means to have sex for the first time). 'You're not a real man until you've done it with a girl,' your mates might tell you. But they're wrong. Being a real man has nothing to do with getting with a girl. Being a man is much more than where your penis has been. For example, *not* having intercourse with your girlfriend because she'd prefer to wait makes you a better brand of man than if you insist on having sex with her.

IT'S OK TO NOT HAVE SeX

You shouldn't *ever* feel that sex is something you *have* to do. If you possibly can, wait until you're older and more mature, because sex for the right reasons and in the right loving relationship will beat sex just for the sake of it every single time.

Do you see what I mean? It's complex, isn't it? And you thought you were going to open this book and just find pictures of people having sex.

Sorry.

tHe 'S' word

From: Disgusted

To: richard_the_wise@hotmail.com

Subject: Noises in the night!
Please explain!

The other night at about 1.00 am, I heard a lot of noise coming from my parents' bedroom. You know, moaning and stuff. It had me a bit worried, to tell you the truth. I thought that maybe Dad's chicken casserole had given Mum a huge stomach ache, the way she was carrying on. Then, after a few minutes, I realised what was going on. They were actually *doing it*! Imagine my horror!

But I have to ask, why all the moaning and other weirdness? Was it all some kind of big performance? What's the story?

Disgusted.

tHe 'S' word

From: richard_the_wise@hotmail.com

To: Disgusted

Subject: Re: Noises in the night!
Please explain!

First, what were you doing awake at that time of the night? I hope it wasn't a school night.

Look, sometimes it's hard to tell the difference between someone moaning and groaning because they've eaten a dodgy curry (like that one I had in Dhaka that time), or moaning and groaning because they're doing something that feels good. Like having sex, for example.

If the sound of your parents having sex is bothering you, try closing your door, or asking them to stop. Actually, now I think about it, just close your door. Your parents having sex is a good thing. It usually means that they

still love each other, which is only ever a good thing. Would you rather they were shouting at each other? No, I didn't think so.

So close your door. And don't be disgusted, Disgusted. It's only natural.

RICHARD THE WISE

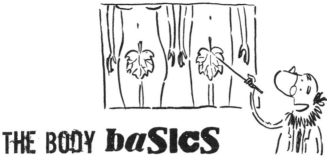

3 THE BODY baSIcS

No - I don't see a worm.

You probably don't remember this, but when your mother took you to playschool as a toddler, you didn't look all that different from the girls that were the same age as you. The things that *did* make you seem different might have been the clothes your parents dressed you in, the way they cut your hair, or the toys they gave you to play with. But just to look at with their clothes on, small boys and small girls are all pretty much the same as each other. Their bodies are roughly the same shape, with smooth faces and flat chests, and no real clue to tell you if they're a boy or a girl.

That is, until they take a bath. You don't need me to tell you that boys and girls are different in one important place — between their legs. Most readers will know what the various bits and pieces are called. But there might be a few who don't, so we should go on a very quick tour.

Being a boy, you'll have noticed the dangly thing between your legs. That's your **penis**. Say hello to your penis. There are a number of other words people use for this useful little device, but since it has a perfectly good real name, we'll just stick to that.

SAY HELLO TO YOUR PENIS

Your penis has a number of functions. It's where your urine comes out, for a start. This is one of the really useful things about being male. When you're out camping or hiking, you can just walk behind a tree and pee against the trunk, standing up the whole time. Girls probably feel a bit envious of this, since they have to sit down to go to the toilet, even for just a pee. So *that's* handy, for a start.

The other function of your penis is for **sexual intercourse**, which is when a man's penis is put inside a woman's body. Some intercourse is for fun, and some is for making babies, but your penis doesn't really care. As far as your penis is concerned, it's all pretty much the same. We'll go over the way the baby-making thing works later, but for now we'll just say that your penis is mostly interested in intercourse.

Under your penis is your **scrotum**, which is a wrinkly little sack of skin. The comedian Billy Connolly says that God made the scrotum out of leftover elbow skin. I don't know if this is true or not, but it is a pretty funny way to describe it. The idea of the scrotum is that it is a place to keep your **testicles**. Some people call testicles *nuts* or *balls*, and if you feel them you'll understand why. What are your testicles for? Your testicles actually produce **sperm**, which are the tiny cells that join with a woman's egg to grow into a baby.

YOUR PENIS IS MOSTLY INTERESTED IN INTERCOURSE

It makes sense that the *penis* is outside the body, but why do the testicles have to be hanging out there in the open, just waiting for a fast-moving football or a well-aimed punch from your little brother? That's because for your sperm to survive they need to remain at just the right temperature. You might have noticed how when it's cold in the swimming pool your testicles shrink up high under your penis, like the wheels of a plane shortly after it has taken off. The

Testicles:
Nature's way of saying pay attention.

truth is they're just trying to stay warm. And when they swing low in the summer breeze, they're trying to stay cool.

Of course, you'll have noticed that girls are different. When boys wear swimming gear, they have a lumpy little package in the front, but girls don't have that. Girls are just kind of smooth and neat and tidy. This is because the bits of a girl's body that make her female are tucked away, and are mostly out of sight. The places where the eggs come from (the **ovaries**) and the place where a growing baby lives until it's old enough to be born (the **uterus**) and the tube that leads up into those parts of her body (the **vagina**) are all very neatly packaged inside a girl, with a nicely hidden opening about where your scrotum is. This opening is covered by lips, called **labia**, and that whole area is known as the **vulva**. At the top of the vulva is a small, sensitive organ called the **clitoris**, and just below that is the **urethra**, which is where the urine comes out.

So those are the main physical differences between young boys and girls. Once **puberty** begins, which is when your body starts to change from being a child to

> tHE BITS OF A GIRL'S BODY THAT MAKE HER FEMALE ARE TUCKED AWAY, AND ARE MOSTLY OUT OF SIGHT

an adult, a few other things become a bit more obvious. So now might be a good time to discuss (drum roll, please) puberty!

From: Soprano

To: richard_the_wise@hotmail.com

Subject: Ouch

Dear Richard the Wise,

The other day I was playing cricket and I got clocked right in the … well, the balls. I wasn't wearing a box, and it really hurt. I fell over and couldn't breathe for a while, and I thought I was going to throw up. (I didn't, but I was close.) Everyone seemed to think it was pretty funny. Everyone except me, that is.

My question is, could I have done any damage to my 'boys'?

Soprano

tHe 'S' word

From: richard_the_wise@hotmail.com

To: Soprano

Subject: Re: Ouch

Dear Soprano,

Sorry, I shouldn't laugh, but it is pretty amusing when someone gets one in the groin. But you're right when you say that it's not very funny for the person writhing on the ground grasping at his private parts and crying.

Yes, you can sustain damage after you've been clocked, but it's usually obvious within a short time. In other words, if you notice anything odd, such as lumps, bleeding, extra swelling or pain that doesn't go away, get it looked at by a doctor.

Oh, and try wearing a protector, or a box, as you called it. It'll still hurt if you get

whacked by a fast inswinger, but nowhere near as much as if you're not wearing one. You goose.

RICHARD THE WISE

4 PUberty

Some kids get scared by puberty. I'm not sure why this is. Maybe they feel pressured by grown-ups who expect them to behave like little adults, or maybe they just enjoy being a kid so much that they don't ever want to grow up.

But really, the changes to your body that come with puberty are nothing to be too afraid of. Besides, they happen to everyone.

But what makes puberty happen? At around the age of ten or eleven (sometimes younger), glands in the body of a boy begin to produce **testosterone**, which is a kind of chemical. Testosterone does a lot of different things. It makes men feel excited about most things to do with sex, it makes them feel strong and brave, it makes them show off around girls, and it sometimes makes them act like complete idiots. But the sudden rush of testosterone at the beginning of puberty also causes a few changes to a boy's body.

First, your body shape starts to change. Your arms and chest and shoulders grow bigger, which causes you to look stronger. Your face might change a bit as well, with your jaw getting squarer. The other way your face changes is that you start growing hair on it. At first it might be just a bit of a fluffy moustache, but then it becomes a whole beard, and before you know it you're locking the bathroom door while you borrow your dad's razor.

Geez, puberty didn't just hit Sam - it ran right over him!

This hairiness isn't just on your face, though. Your legs and arms might become hairier, and your chest will start growing thick curly hairs. But even that's not all. The area around your penis and testicles, and part-way up your stomach, will gradually get a pretty heavy growth of thick, curly hairs. This is called **pubic hair**.

'So I'm going to be hairier,' you say. 'That's OK, as long as that's everything. And as long as I don't start looking like a werewolf.'

Well it's not quite everything, but it's still nothing to panic about. Before puberty, both boys and girls have fairly high voices. But once puberty begins, a boy's voice gets deeper. At first it might be a gradual thing, followed by a kind of halfway stage where one minute you'll be talking in a deep, manly voice and the next you'll be talking in a kind of high squeak. But eventually you'll have a constant voice that won't crack just as you stand up to read your science report to the class.

When puberty starts, you might get **acne**. The other word for acne is *pimples* or *spots*. Again, this is totally normal and happens because of testosterone and other chemicals.

Lastly, your brain changes a bit. You might begin to have mood swings, and find that one minute you feel fantastic and the next you feel sad or angry for no reason. This can be really confusing, especially if you don't know why it's happening. Your brain is changing and learning to look at life in a different, more mature way. You might find that you fight with your parents a lot more as well. You're growing up into an adult, and you're finding out how to live in a grown-up

July 22nd - the day Joel woke up with Puberty.

Excuse me - have you seen my son?

Whatever...

world. (Parents find this hard as well, by the way. It can be quite tricky watching your kids heading into puberty. To your parents, almost everything you do looks like a mistake, and it also reminds them that they're getting older.)

PUBERTY HAPPENS TO GIRLS TOO, BUT OF COURSE THE CHANGES ARE DIFFERENT

Puberty happens to girls too, but of course the changes are different. Girls start to grow breasts, their hips get wider, and they start to grow pubic hair as well. They also start to **menstruate**. Sometimes girls call this *getting their period*. They don't like to discuss this with boys, because they can find it a bit embarrassing, but just so you'll know, there'll be more about periods in the section about making babies.

So that's a quick look at the way your body changes. Some of these changes might have already started. Just remember, every man you see went through puberty, and just like you they all felt weird at some stage. So try to relax; it'll be OK. You're becoming a man, and even though being a man is more than just having a hairy face and a deep voice, those things are a part of it. They're also completely normal and natural. That's a comforting thought to keep in mind.

From: Screechy

To: richard_the_wise@hotmail.com

Subject: My voice! Aaargh! Help!

Dear Richard the Wise,

My voice hasn't quite broken yet. Most of the other boys in my class have already got nice, deep voices, but I'm still talking in a high one. The other day I said something to my friend Harry while Mr Blayney had his back turned to the class, and he goes, 'Girls, I can hear you talking.' Which sucks, if he can't tell the difference between my voice and a girl's voice.

So when will my voice break?

Screechy

the 'S' word

Dear Screechy,

Have you heard of Murphy's Law? Murphy's Law states that if anything bad can go wrong it will, and at the worst possible time. If this law is to be believed, I predict that your voice will start to break at the beginning of a school term, just so everyone else can enjoy the entire journey with you. It will *not* happen over the Christmas holidays, of that much I can assure you. That would be too easy, finishing school with a voice like Bart Simpson's and coming back several weeks later sounding more like Principal Skinner.

But it's not the end of the world, because out of a class of thirty students about half

will be boys (all of them if you're at a boys'
school, obviously), and there's a good chance
that at least some of those boys are going
through the same thing as you *right now*,
with their voices cracking and failing and
squeaking along with yours. And best of all,
one hundred percent of the boys in your class
will go through it at some stage.

So don't worry about it, dude. Have a
laugh. The world's not about to end. Just
don't volunteer to read out the sports results
at assembly until you're sure you can get
through it without hitting high-C.

RICHARD THE WISE

5   SeX: HOW IT WORKS

It's true — your penis only cares about one thing: sex. Or maybe we should use the proper term, which is **sexual intercourse**. And basically there are two reasons for intercourse. One is for making babies; the other is a way for two people who really care about each other to get extra close. You could call this 'sex for fun', and we're going to talk about the fun bit in a minute. But first we should put on our white lab-coats and talk about the scientific, baby-making bit.

About once a month a woman's body releases an **ovum**, or an egg. This egg is a lot smaller than the chicken eggs you eat for breakfast. In fact, you need a microscope to see a human ovum clearly. A woman has her lifetime supply of **ova** already in her ovaries when she's born, but she releases them one by one, usually one every four weeks or so, from when she gets to puberty until the eggs run out, which usually happens when she's between forty-five and fifty-five years old.

Once the egg is released, it starts heading down a narrow tube into the **uterus** (also known as the **womb**). It's hoping to meet a man's sperm heading in the opposite direction, and if it does it will sometimes be **fertilised** by that sperm. The name for this is **conception**, which means that a new life is formed.

Once an egg is fertilised, it starts growing into a baby. This is a complicated and amazing process, where a cell splits and becomes two, then those two split again, and so on. To get an idea of how this works, take a sheet of paper and tear it in half. Put those pieces together and tear them in half. Put those four pieces together and tear them again. If you do this several times, you'll soon have many, many little pieces of paper.

In the same way, when a fertilised egg divides, two becomes four, then eight, then sixteen, then thirty-two, sixty-four, 128, 256, 512, 1024, and on and on, until the number is in the millions.

If this whole fertilisation thing happens, the baby — which at this stage is called an **embryo** — settles into place against the wall of the uterus. Then, if everything goes well, about forty weeks or nine months later the baby is born, usually by coming down the vagina, or sometimes by a doctor performing an operation to remove the baby from the uterus.

> IF EVERYTHING GOES WELL, ABOUT FORTY WEEKS OR NINE MONTHS LATER THE BABY IS BORN

Most of the time the egg won't meet a sperm coming the other way. It will travel down the tube into the uterus, find nothing there, and die. That's when the lining of the uterus, which was ready and waiting for a freshly fertilised egg, peels away and comes out of the vagina. This looks like blood, and it lasts for a few days. This is **menstruation**, or a *period*. During their periods women have to do all kinds of secretive stuff that they don't like boys to know about. It's best you don't tease girls about this kind of thing. If you do, don't expect them to ever talk to you again. Seriously.

So that's how a baby is **conceived** and begins to grow. The one bit we haven't talked about yet is how the man's sperm gets into the woman's uterus, so let's do that now.

When a man and a woman have intercourse, a couple of things happen. First, the man gets excited (or **aroused**), and his penis gets hard. This is called an

erection, which is caused by blood being pumped into the blood vessels in the penis. Erections can be a bit embarrassing, particularly during puberty, because they can be difficult to hide, especially inside swimming gear or sports shorts. And, unfortunately, they can arrive at the worst possible moment, like when you're about to get off the bus at school, or when you're walking to the summer camp bathroom in your pyjamas, or when your mum pulls your blankets down in the morning.

At least steer me in the right direction.

So back to our happy couple. The man's got an erection, and at the same time the woman's getting excited too. For her, getting excited means that her vagina is getting moist and slippery, and ready for intercourse.

Then, when they're both ready, they lie close together, and the man slides his penis into the woman's vagina. You might find it hard to believe, but this feels very good, and usually the man slides his penis in and out again and again, which also feels good. This can go on for a little while or for a long time, but eventually the man reaches the point where he **climaxes** or has an **orgasm**, which is a very exciting all-over tingling feeling. Usually when a man climaxes he also

ejaculates, which means that **semen** squirts from the end of his penis, from the same hole that his urine usually comes out of. Semen is a thick, white, creamy substance that contains millions of sperm cells, which have been created in the testicles. Once the semen is ejaculated into the woman's vagina, the sperm all start swimming like crazy. If you could look at some sperm under a microscope, you'd see that they look a lot like tiny tadpoles, using their tails to swim up into the uterus, hoping to meet a lonely egg coming the other way.

Remember, even though there are millions of sperm cells, there is usually only one egg, so you won't get millions of babies. Except for rare cases where identical twins start to grow, you'll only get as many babies as there are eggs.

But what if there's *no* egg? In that case, nothing happens. Those sperm just swim around, totally unaware that there was never any egg to race to in the first place. And eventually they die.

When it's all explained and you think about all the things that have to go right, it's actually pretty amazing that anyone is ever born. But babies are born every day. There are over six billion people in the world right now. That's six

Man - I'm pooped!

Do you think there really is an egg?

thousand million, or six thousand thousand thousand. That means that six billion times an egg and a sperm have met, joined, and formed a baby, and often this process of conception happens completely by accident. Like I said in the first chapter, that's a lot of sex.

THERE ARE OVER SIX BILLION PEOPLE IN THE WORLD RIGHT NOW. THAT'S SIX THOUSAND MILLION, OR SIX THOUSAND THOUSAND THOUSAND

From: Trekkie

To: richard_the_wise@hotmail.com

Subject: Dreams

Dear Richard the Wise,

Sometimes at night I have a dream about a particular girl. I haven't met her, because she's just this girl off a TV show. But in my dream she takes off all her clothes, and then we start kissing and that, and then I get this weird kind of feeling, and when I wake up my pyjama pants are all wet in the front. Is it normal to wet the bed when you dream about babes?

Trekkie

From: richard_the_wise@hotmail.com

To: Trekkie

Subject: Re: Dreams

Dear Trekkie,

The good news is that you're not wetting the bed, at least not in the normal sense. What you're having is a 'wet dream', which is something that men of any age can have but that boys your age experience more often. Basically your brain is playing a trick on you; it makes you believe that you are actually getting cosy with that Star Trek 'babe' you mentioned. And the crazy thing is that the tricks don't end there. Sometimes it's not the humanoid Star Trek babe but the Klingon babe. Or it might be your teacher, or the woman who works at the service station. Don't be alarmed, though; it's just your brain practising at being sexually aroused.

Oh, and the wet spot you mentioned? It's semen. Yes, my friend, you've ejaculated in your sleep. The good news is that everything seems to be working perfectly. The bad news is that you weren't awake to enjoy it.

Live long and prosper.

RICHARD THE WISE

Talking about sex and intercourse in a mechanical way doesn't make it sound like very much fun. You could easily find out everything you need to know by reading an encyclopaedia. But the problem with learning that way is that an encyclopaedia only tells you about the bare facts. *During intercourse, the male places his penis in the vagina of the female, which is pleasurable for both.* This doesn't make it sound very pleasurable at all. It makes it sound more like the instructions for putting together an Ikea coffee-table.

So we should talk about the emotional side of sex, which is just as important as penises and vaginas, maybe even more important.

There is some intercourse that isn't nice at all. If someone is having sex because they feel they have to, or if they feel that they'll be hurt or bullied or harmed if they don't, that's not going to be pleasant. In fact, it will be awful. As discussed earlier, often young people are told by their friends that they're not normal if they don't 'do it'. And sometimes a boy will tell his girlfriend that having sex with him is the only way to prove that she loves him. If someone demands sex from another person as proof of their love, it's not a very healthy brand of love to begin with. It's probably not love at all.

IF SOMEONE DEMANDS SeX FROM ANOTHER PERSON AS PROOF OF THEIR LOVE. IT'S PROBABLY NOT LOVE AT ALL

The best sex anyone can have is the kind that happens when two people really care about each other. That kind of sex includes the warm and exciting emotions that come with feeling close and loved. The other kind — sex that is just for the sake of having an orgasm — is not the best kind, and in fact it often ends up being pretty disappointing, even damaging.

Some people believe that you should be married to the person you have sex with, others think you should at least be in a long relationship, and others think that it's OK to have sex with someone you just know fairly well. And there are some who also believe that it's fine to have intercourse with a person you've only just met, even on the same day that you first meet them. But that's where all the emotional stuff becomes important. Sex with someone you've only just met is not going to have any of that emotional side to it, and it's almost certainly going to be disappointing. You're also going to feel pretty awful and maybe even ashamed the next day, when you realise that you have shared such an amazing thing with a person who's practically a stranger.

tHE FIRST TIME

Let's talk about '**losing your virginity**'. Because of the way intercourse is shown in movies and on television, we expect that the first time will be amazingly good. But sadly it often isn't. For a girl, the first time can be uncomfortable, even painful, and some young men get so excited the first time that they ejaculate almost

This is my first time - how about you?

Nah... I've taken my clothes off heaps of times...

straightaway. But just like anything, sex is something that you get better at after you've done it a few times.

Having sex with someone is a little different from when you **masturbate** (which means playing with or stroking your penis). For a start, there's someone else in the room with you, and you don't want to do it wrong, or badly. So you become a bit nervous. And of course there's the fact that you mightn't have seen each other without clothes on before, and that can often be enough to make you both feel a bit weird and uncomfortable.

When you start having sex is up to you, and it's something you should think about very carefully. Perhaps you could talk to someone you trust, like your parents or an older brother, a teacher, a school counsellor, or your doctor. But what is really important is that you only ever have intercourse for the right reasons, not because you feel that you owe it to the other person, or because you think that they owe it to you. Sex is a very special thing, so you should treat it that way, sharing it only with someone you really care about. Remember too that the older you are when you start

to have sex, the more mature you'll be, and the better you'll be able to handle all the tricky emotions that are attached to sex.

SEX IS A VERY SPECIAL THING, SO YOU SHOULD TREAT IT THAT WAY

HOW FAR IS OK?

But it's not just the emotions that are tricky. Sometimes it gets hard to know what is OK physically and what isn't. Is it all right to do one thing with a girl, but not OK to do something else? Where are the lines and boundaries, and how can you work it all out?

By the time many boys are at the end of primary school, they'll have held hands with a girl, and maybe even kissed her. You might even have been 'going out' with someone. Then, as puberty starts to really get going, you find yourself looking at girls a lot more, admiring the shape of their bodies, flirting a bit, and thinking about them all the time.

Then you might start feeling interested in one particular girl, and you start talking to her a bit more, and you could even decide that you want to 'ask her out'. For a lot of kids this doesn't actually involve going anywhere: it just means that she's your girlfriend and you're her boyfriend. It also means that you're spending a lot of time with that one girl.

But suddenly it gets pretty awkward. When you hold hands with a girl or even just sit next to her on the bus, you might find that you're getting an erection. This can be embarrassing, but what your body is telling you is that it's interested in intercourse.

You might also get this sudden desire to touch her body. (Obviously you'd only do this if she were comfortable with it; you can't just go around touching girls. People get arrested for that kind of thing!) To start with you might just feel like stroking her arms, then her face, but after a while you'll notice that girls' bodies are amazing things, soft and smooth and curvy and warm. This is no accident. Our male minds can't help noticing bodies that are soft and smooth and curvy and warm. This is all part of sex as well.

OUR MALE MINDS CAN'T HELP NOTICING BODIES THAT ARE SOFT AND SMOOTH AND CURVY AND WARM

Sometimes young people first start having sexual experiences just by touching. They might like to spend time alone together touching each other's bodies. Once they start touching each other in a way that makes them very excited, they're having a kind of sex, even if his penis doesn't go anywhere near her vagina. They might not think that they're actually 'having sex', but it is very similar, and often people find it very hard to stop at that point, and they keep going until they're having proper intercourse.

So how do you know when to stop and when it's OK to keep going?

Really, it's all about communicating with the person you're with. Sometimes this means that you might touch her in a particular way, or try to kiss her, and she'll show you that she's not comfortable with that. She might do this by pushing your hand away or pulling back from you, or by making some other obvious sign. Just because she doesn't actually say 'Stop it. I don't like that' doesn't mean that she's fine with what you're doing.

Of course, if she does ask you to stop, you must *always* stop. You should never force someone to do something that they're uncomfortable with. And it might surprise you to know that sometimes girls force themselves on guys as well, and if that happens, it's perfectly fine for you to ask her to stop too.

The other thing you can do is actually ask if what you're doing is all right. 'Are you OK with this?' is a good way to check, and if she says 'Yes', then you know. But if she says 'No', then you shouldn't go any further. Instead of just saying 'No', she might say 'Let's just hold hands for a bit longer' or 'I liked what we were doing before'. And you should respect the way she feels. As well as being the right thing to do, she'll also think a lot more of you for behaving that way.

IT'S NEVER OK TO FORCE SOMEONE TO HAVE Sex

Remember, it's *never* OK to force someone to have sex — through pressuring them, threatening them, hurting them or by using your strength. It's disrespectful and cruel, and it's also breaking the law.

With all this talk about knowing how far is OK, and knowing when to stop, you might be wondering how old you have to be to have sex, either as intercourse or as the other things discussed.

Once again, the older you are, the more mature you tend to be. This will mean that you can deal better with the complex emotional stuff that comes along with sex. As far as the law goes, the age of consent in Ireland and Northern Ireland is 17; this means it's illegal to have sex before you're 17. In the UK the age of consent is 16. If you want to know more about these laws, you should discuss it with an adult you trust, like your school counsellor, and they can help you find out.

I think the best rule is this one: if you're in doubt or not sure, just *don't do it*. Sex is wonderful when it's done right, but if it's done for the wrong reasons it can mess things up in a pretty major way. For a long time, maybe for your entire life.

From: Busting_to_go

To: richard_the_wise@hotmail.com

Subject: Is it time?

IF YOU'RE IN DOUBT OR NOT SURE, JUST DON'T DO IT

Dear Richard the Wise,

I've been going out with my girlfriend for almost two years now. (We're both 14.) Everything I've read says that you should only have sex with someone if you love them. And we do love each other. We've been mucking around a bit for a while now, but I think we're ready to 'do it'.

So is it OK to go ahead? My mates reckon it's time, but I wanted to know what you think.

Mr Keen

the 'S' word

Dear Mr Keen,

First, why do you want to complicate things just for the sake of having intercourse anyway?
Is it because it seems like a grown-up thing to do? Are you worried that she doesn't know how much you love her? There are heaps of ways you can show her *that* without having sex — ways that won't turn you into a 15-year-old dad, with a girlfriend who has to leave school to look after your baby.

Besides, you say that *you* think you're ready to go all the way. And apparently your friends are pretty sure the time is right. But what does *she* think? Have you talked to *her* about it? What's her opinion? Or doesn't that matter as much as your mates'?

Why not wait? It is OK *not* to have sex, you know. And so what if your mates tease you? It's none of their business.

Yes, sex is fun, but it's not something you should rush into. Seriously, dude.

Out,

RICHARD THE WISE

PS: If you do decide to ignore this good advice and have sex with your girlfriend, at least wear a condom.

6 intercourse,
AND WHAT IT'S really LIKE

An earlier chapter talked about intercourse, why it happens, and how it happens. Let's go over it all again, but in a bit more detail.

Men can be ready for intercourse at almost any time, and this is because of the way we're made. A woman's eggs are in the right place to meet sperm for only a couple of days every month, so if any babies are going to be born at all, the sperm needs to be there at just the right time. This means that the man needs to be able to get his sperm close to the egg very quickly, and without much warning. This is why boys only have to think about sex, or see a sexy picture, or brush up against a girl who they think is nice, and they can get an

Um... he said six _not_ sex. This is a maths lesson after all.

erection. And once you've got an erection, you're pretty much ready to have intercourse. Physically, anyway.

But women are made differently, and they need more time to get ready to have sex.

Do you remember how I said that sex is more than just two naked people lying close together? It's really about two people showing how they feel about each other. (Sometimes intercourse is also called **making love**, which is quite a good way to describe it.)

SOMETIMES INTERCOURSE IS ALSO CALLED MAKING LOVE

This is why **foreplay** is important. Foreplay basically means what it sounds like: play *before* sex. That doesn't mean that couples get out the PSP or the X-Box, or the Monopoly board. It means that they take time doing all that lovey-dovey stuff, like kissing, cuddling and holding hands. Some couples like to take days just spending time together, talking, touching and that sort of thing. Being romantic, I guess you could call it.

And men don't need to worry about doing something with that erection before it goes down. They can wait for ages without actually having intercourse, and sometimes if they wait a while it's better once they get around to doing it.

So what else can foreplay be? It's not just holding hands beside the sea or having candles on the dinner table. Mood is very important, but eventually a couple is going to have to actually touch each other.

Cuddling is important. Girls really like cuddles with someone they love, and even if you don't think cuddling is for you, you should try it. It can actually be a lot of fun.

Of course, kissing is a big one. I don't know why, but kissing someone on the mouth is a very exciting and sexy thing to do. (Provided that you like that person and they like you back, of course. Kissing your best mate for a dare is neither exciting nor sexy. It's just awful. So I'm told.)

But the human body is sensitive in all sorts of other places apart from the mouth. The **genitals** (your penis and testicles, her vagina and vulva) are really sensitive, of course, but so are the nipples and the breasts (men's nipples are ticklish too, you know), the armpits and the inside of the thighs. The back and the stomach, the neck, the face and the ears are all very sensitive as well, and stroking, kissing, licking or nibbling those places will make a person feel very excited. And the

It was clear from the start that Jeremy's kissing technique needed some tweaking...

longer two people do it, the more excited they will both become.

When foreplay has gone on for a while, both people's bodies will be ready. This means that the man has an erection (still!) and the woman's vagina is very moist and slippery. This is a good sign that they're both ready for what most people think is the most exciting bit of sex — intercourse.

DRAIN EQUALS GREAT BIG SEX ORGAN

There are a few ways that a man and a woman can get in position for intercourse, but often it's done with the woman lying on her back with her legs apart, and the man lying on top of her, between her legs. This is a perfect position for his penis to slide into her vagina, and once it's in there, he'll usually move it in and out. This feels really good, not just because of how it makes his penis feel, but because this is the closest that two people can ever be. Being close together, they can also see how nice it feels for each other, and that makes it even more exciting. Brain equals great big sex organ, remember?

There are other positions as well, such as the man lying on his back and the woman sitting on top of him. Whatever position is used, the usual way to have intercourse is to make the penis slide in and out of the vagina. After a while — it could be a minute or less, it could be half an hour or more — the man starts to feel a very strong, tingling feeling all over. This is the beginning of the climax or orgasm mentioned earlier. Once an orgasm starts it can be very hard to stop, and it usually arrives at the same time as the man ejaculates.

Women can have orgasms as well, either before or during intercourse. When a woman has an orgasm, it's a bit different from a man's. She doesn't ejaculate, although she does get the same all-over tingly rush. Some women can have several orgasms in a row, while most men have only one before they feel like a rest. Some women never have an orgasm at all, even though they still enjoy sex, and some have orgasms only when they masturbate, which is when a woman touches or rubs her vulva or clitoris.

After the man has had an orgasm, it can be difficult for him to keep having intercourse. It could be because his erection goes down, or his penis becomes extra sensitive, or he might just not feel like it any more.

This is another way that women are different. After sex, most men like to roll over and go to sleep, a bit like a male lion lying in the sun, while women like to cuddle. This might just be the way we're made, but for men the actual intercourse can feel like the main part of sex, while for women sex can be more about feeling close to someone they like a lot.

The most important thing is this: the best kind of intercourse happens when both people want it, and when both take the time to make the other feel good, rather than just taking whatever they can for themselves. Good sex is shared sex.

From: Pup-tent

To: richard_the_wise@hotmail.com

Subject: Unwanted excitement

Dear Richard the Wise,

The other day in P.E. we were doing exercises, and we had to do sit-ups, and I got partnered with this girl who's kind of nice, but I don't like her or anything. So anyway, she went first while I held her feet. And it was kind of embarrassing, because while I held her feet and watched her doing her sit-ups, I started getting a stiffy. You know, an erection, even though I don't really like her. Not like that, anyway. But then we had to swap, which meant that I had to lie down while she held my feet. Except I had the erection, and I knew that when I lay down she'd see it, and so would everyone else. So I sat up and said I had a sore back, and the teacher got angry with me and put me on detention for not cooperating.

But I didn't even particularly like this girl, so why did I get an erection?

Pup-tent

From: richard_the_wise@hotmail.com

To: Pup-tent

Subject: Re: Unwanted excitement

Dear Pup-tent,

Yep, that does sound like an awful experience. I guess the main thing you want to know is why you got excited in the middle of P.E. class, which is a totally un-sexy kind of place.

Think of it this way: your shuttle needs to be ready for blastoff at a moment's notice, and until Mission Control is confident that it can do so, it keeps running tests. It's a bit like a rehearsal for launch day. Unfortunately, early in the program your shuttle doesn't really communicate with Mission Control very well. In other words, your brain knows that it's a test run, but your penis doesn't, right up until the message finally gets through that there's not going to be a launch today.

And why did it happen around a girl you don't even like? Hey, it's a girl, isn't it? Yeah, but a girl you don't even like that much? I guess that message is still getting through from Mission Control.

Houston, you have no problem.

RICHARD THE WISE

7 Safe SEX

Safe sex isn't two people doing it in a doorway during an avalanche. Safe sex is the name given to all those things you do to protect yourself when you have sex, and we're not talking about helmets or suits of armour.

BIRTH CONTROL

The first thing you might want to protect yourself from is the making of a baby, or **getting pregnan**t. It might seem to you that it's hard to get pregnant, since the egg is around for only a couple of days a month. But the fact is that a lot of babies are conceived totally by accident. This isn't always a bad thing, but often it's not a good thing.

Couples who want to have children are usually already living together. They might feel like their family would be more complete if there was a kid around, or if they already have children they might want more. But many couples want to be able to have sex without worrying about a baby coming along in nine months. Babies cost a lot of money to care for, they take up a lot of your time, and if the woman has a job it might mean that she can't work for a while. Or maybe the two people don't know if they're ready to have children yet, for a lot of different reasons. So couples who want to have sex but don't want a baby need a way to stop the man's sperm reaching that lonely egg. The name for this is **birth control** or **contraception**.

There are a few ways that this can be done. The most common way is with a **condom**. A condom is a bit like a long rubber balloon which fits over the penis, once the man has an erection. Because the rubber is so thin, intercourse still feels good. But when the man ejaculates, all the semen and sperm are caught in a little space at the end of

Raymond was having so much fun blowing up the bag of condoms he didn't realise his date for the evening had left.

the condom, which means that even if there is an egg waiting the sperm can't get to it.

I'm hoping tonight's the night - my wallet weighs a ton!

Condoms are good because they're small and easy to carry around, they're quick to put on, and you don't have to plan as much as you do with some of the other methods of contraception. They're also really good at stopping pregnancy. They're not perfect, but they're very good.

Another way to avoid making a baby is with **the pill**. The pill is a small tablet that the woman takes every day, and it changes the chemicals in her body so that she stops releasing an egg every month. This means that even if sperm get into the woman's uterus, there's no egg there to fertilise.

The pill is also pretty good at stopping babies being made, but like the condom it's not perfect. It can also be a bit of a nuisance, because it means that the woman has to go to a doctor and a chemist to get the tablets, and she has to remember to take her pill every day, other-wise it won't work and she can get pregnant if she has intercourse.

There are a couple of other methods. **Diaphragms**, **sponges** and **spermicidal jelly** are all things that a woman can put into her vagina before she has sex. Most doctors would recommend using the spermicide along with the diaphragm or sponge, just to be extra safe. Spermicide alone is not effective as a contraceptive. These methods stop sperm getting up to where the egg is, but a lot of women don't like to use them, because they're a bit fiddly and messy to use and they have to be used very carefully or they may not work perfectly.

IT TAKES ONLY ONE LITTLE SPERM CELL AND ONE LITTLE EGG TO MAKE ONE LITTLE BABY!

Another method you may have heard of is the **withdrawal method**, which means that the man pulls his penis out of the woman's vagina just before he ejaculates. This is a very unreliable method; it may sometimes work, but it can be difficult for the man to make himself pull out. Also, sometimes a few sperm can escape from the end of his penis before he actually ejaculates. And really, it takes only one little sperm cell and one little egg to make one little baby!

Some religions teach that you should only have sex when you're trying to have a baby, and there are some that teach that using anything at all — such as a condom — to stop a baby being made is wrong. That's for each person and each couple to make up their own mind about.

But, of course, the best way to avoid making a baby is not to have intercourse at all. If a couple doesn't actually have intercourse, it's very difficult for them to get pregnant. It can happen, but usually only with the help of scientists in white lab-coats. Generally speaking, not having intercourse is the best, surest and simplest way to prevent Mr Sperm from meeting Miss Ova.

IF A DISEASE IS HARD TO SPELL THEN YOU PROBABLY DON'T WANT IT!

SEXUALLY TRANSMITTED DISEASES

The second part of safe sex has to do with **sexually transmitted diseases (STDs)**. There are quite a few of these nasty little surprises out there. Some of them might just cause a bit of an itch on your penis, and some can stop you ever having children at all, even when you want to. And the worst kinds of STDs can make you really sick, or even kill you. A good rule is that if a disease is hard to spell then you probably don't want it! Some of the names of these diseases are herpes, hepatitis, chlamydia, syphilis and gonorrhoea (see what I mean?). Plus there's the big one, which is HIV/AIDS, which is easier to spell than the others but much worse than all of them. There are a few ways you can catch HIV (the virus that causes AIDS) but the most common way is by having sexual intercourse with someone who already has it.

The trouble is you can't always tell if someone has one of these diseases just by looking at them or talking to them. They might already have a disease that they've picked up from someone else they've had sex with before, but if they don't look very sick you won't know until you get it yourself.

The best way to avoid catching anything from someone you have sex with (or to avoid giving them any bug that *you* might have) is to wear a condom. The pill, diaphragms and sponges won't stop diseases; they'll only stop you from making a baby. So if you want to be as safe as you can be, you should use a condom.

But remember, the only way to be totally sure that you won't get anything nasty from someone is not to have sex with them in the first place. *Then* you'll be safe.

And if there is something about your health that worries you, go to a doctor. Health problems that are treated early are most likely to respond well. And it's important to know that a doctor isn't allowed to talk to anyone else about your problems without your

permission. So whatever you say to your doctor is completely private.

From: Nervous

To: richard_the_wise@hotmail.com

Subject: Advice needed please

Dear Richard the Wise,

How do I buy a condom, and how do I put one on?

Nervous

PS: Will this use up all of my pocket-money?

From: richard_the_wise@hotmail.com

To: Nervous

Subject: Re: Advice needed please

Dear Nervous,

You can get condoms from supermarkets and chemists. It's not that tricky, you know. You pick up the packet, take it to the front counter and pay for it. Don't even think about putting it on until you're safely at home with the door closed — shop security guys can tend to get a bit cranky about that kind of thing.

How do you put it on? It comes rolled up and flat, and you put it at the end of your erect penis and roll it down. And afterwards, when you've finished having intercourse, you take the condom off and put it in the bin. The instructions in the pack say that you shouldn't flush it down the toilet, and that you shouldn't send it back to the manufacturer. Like you would! Now *there's* a package you don't want to get in the mail!

One more thing, Nervous. Anyone who has to ask how to buy a condom is probably a bit young to be needing one in the first place. And anyone who is still getting pocket-money

Um...hi...yeah, look, I was just, ah... wondering where y'know, if it was all right with you, if you could tell me, um, ah, where the co...co... co... ah, cough lollies were?

is *certainly* too young. So think about it carefully, dude. Maybe you should spend that pocket-money on another date. Don't rush in. I mean it. There's plenty of time for that kind of thing later.

But if you must rush in, a condom's a good idea. In other words, if you must do it, best that you do it safely.

RICHARD THE WISE

PS: Near the toothpastes and shampoos.

8 bIts & bObs

This chapter discusses a few other things to do with sex that you might have wondered about from time to time.

MASTURBATION

Masturbation is when you 'play with yourself' or touch your own genitals because it feels good. It's also sometimes called 'wanking', 'jerking off' or 'tossing off', plus about a hundred other names. Some boys first start playing with their penis when they're babies; others don't start until they're older. Some men and boys say they've never done it, but most of them are probably lying. Almost every male masturbates at some time in his life. The American comedian Lily Tomlin says that men first started walking on their hind legs so that their hands would be free for masturbating. Of course that's not true, but she's right when she suggests that practically all men masturbate. And it might surprise you to know that most girls and women masturbate as well.

Masturbation isn't something that people talk about very much. That's mostly because it's something done in private, and also because it's been seen for a very long time as something to be ashamed of. Boys and men used to be told that if they masturbated they would go blind, the palms of their hands would get hairy, and they'd find it hard to pay attention in class. None of these things are true. In fact, masturbation actually teaches you a lot about your body, sex, and some of those feelings that happen during intercourse. For those reasons it's normal and actually quite healthy.

Of course, just like anything, if you do nothing but masturbate you'll eventually become very boring. But when it's something you do sometimes rather than at every possible waking moment, there's nothing at all wrong with it. And if it did cause blindness,

SOME MEN AND BOYS SAY THEY'VE NEVER DONE IT, BUT MOST OF THEM ARE PROBABLY LYING

One TUG too MANy.

there'd be rather a lot of men and boys walking around with white canes and guide dogs!

People masturbate in different ways, but for most it involves stroking or rubbing your erect penis, usually until you ejaculate.

Why do people do it? Is there some psychological reason to do with loving yourself? No, it's probably just because it feels good, and that's it. It's not about feeling close to someone you like, or sharing emotions or being romantic or loving. It's just for pleasure, with nothing else to think or worry about. And provided you do it in private, it won't hurt anyone.

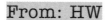

From: HW

To: richard_the_wise@hotmail.com

Subject: About wanking

Hiya Richard the Wise,

What's your best advice about masturbation?

HW

From: richard_the_wise@hotmail.com

To: HW

Subject: Re: About wanking

Dear HW,

What do you want me to say? Do you want instructions? Should I draw you a diagram? I'm really not sure how to answer this question, so I'll just say this: *do it somewhere private*. In your bedroom is fine. In the bathroom with the door locked is no problem. But in the biology section of your school library during lunch break — now that's not such a good look. This kind of behaviour can lead to name-calling that can last for a very long time. Bad, *bad* name-calling. Into adulthood. Until you die.

RICHARD THE WISE

PORNOGRAPHY

Pornography (or **porn**) is anything that shows or talks about sex, or things concerning sex, in a way that's only meant to make the viewer or reader sexually excited. So a textbook that shows naked people isn't pornography, and this book isn't pornography, because its purpose is to give you information rather than make you feel excited.

Some examples of pornography are magazines that show naked or partly-dressed people in poses that are obviously sexual, videos or DVDs that show people having sex, or books that describe sex in a particular way. The Internet has made the job of parents and teachers quite tricky, because it's made pornography very easy to get hold of, even for really young children.

Turtle porn

A lot of pornography distorts sex as a loving expression between two people who are close and makes it into a pretty nasty kind of thing, showing people doing things that two loving people might never dream of doing with each other. That kind of porn is easy to recognise, but sometimes the line between art and pornography isn't very clear at all. This isn't a new problem. Hundreds of years ago, paintings that some people have called art were called porn by others. This has happened with books as well. And one person might look at a nude photo and be totally sure that it's art, while someone else might come along and say, 'I'm not comfortable with someone showing that much skin — this is pornography.'

But most of the time porn is pretty easy to spot. And when you see porn, you might get an erection and feel excited. This is natural, since men are designed to be ready for intercourse very soon after something — anything — makes them start thinking about sex.

SOMETIMES THE LINE BETWEEN ART AND PORNOGRAPHY ISN'T VERY CLEAR AT ALL

Looking at pictures of naked people is something that curious boys (and men) have done for a very long time. Some people say that it helps young men learn about women, while others say that it makes women seem unimportant, and leads boys to think that they don't need to respect women at all.

Maybe you could think of it this way: most porn is made for men by men, and because of that the women in a lot of the pictures aren't shown much respect. Of course there are some women who allow themselves to be photographed or filmed in this way, knowing exactly what they're doing and getting paid a lot of money for it. But there are also a lot of models who do it because they need money, acceptance or love, and there are some who don't want to pose at all and are being forced to do so. And the problem is that sometimes it's hard to tell the difference between the ones who want to be in those kinds of photos or videos and those who don't.

One thing that is *never* OK is porn that has kids in it. Not only are children too young to be taking part in such things, they're inevitably being forced into it. This means that these children are learning about sex in a way that is unhealthy, and are being hurt in many different ways. Anyone who is caught making or keeping child porn can go to jail for a very long time, and if you know of anyone who has it or is trying to sell it, you should let someone responsible know immediately.

From: Embarrassed

To: richard_the_wise@hotmail.com

Subject: Is this porn?

Dear Richard the Wise,

Sometimes I get an erection when I look at the models in my sister's fashion magazines.

Then I feel like going back to my room and …
well, you know … masturbating. What should
I do?

Embarrassed

PS: Is this pornography?

From: richard_the_wise@hotmail.com

To: Embarrassed

Subject: Re: Is this porn?

Dear Embarrassed,

First I was going to ask why you were looking
at your sister's fashion magazines in the first
place. Then I was going to ask what you were
doing in her room at all, and if she knew that
you'd been looking at her magazines. Then
I thought, maybe he's looking at his sister's
magazines *because* he finds the models
exciting. And I don't blame you —— some of

those girls are really sexy. But I wouldn't call those kinds of magazines pornographic, no, even if they *do* make you want to dash back to your room for a bit of private affection.

What should you do? Hey, I don't think it matters too much what I say, because you and I both know that you're going to keep doing what you're doing anyway. So my best advice is this: don't get caught in your sister's room, especially with your hand stuck down your pants. And if you are busted looking at the bikini edition of *Girlzone*, just tell her that you're researching lycra for a science project. Or something. It doesn't matter what you say, because she's not going to believe you.

But it's worth a try.

Happy reading,

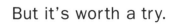

RICHARD THE WISE

BEING GAY

If you were planning to skip this bit because you think you already know about gay people, or you don't *want* to know about gay people, I really think you should read it. You might learn something new.

What a wonderfully gay day.

What a queer thing to say!

Gay used to mean 'happy'. Then the term changed and came to stand for men who are attracted to other men rather than women. Then, because of that, it turned into a word some people use to describe something that is bad or lame: 'The wheels on that car are like *so* gay!' This is a shame, because using it in that way also suggests that all gay people are bad or lame, which isn't true.

Gay or **homosexual** people are men who prefer men, or women who prefer women (also called **lesbians**). It isn't even always about sexual intercourse. There are gay people who never have intercourse at all but are just attracted to the same sex, just like **straight** people are attracted to the opposite sex.

Why are some people gay? Some might be born that way, others might become gay because of past experiences, or both. The reasons are complex, but no matter what they might be, there are some myths — or untruths — that are still widely believed about gay people.

- **Myth 1:** *Gay people are all perverts.* When we use the word pervert we imagine people skulking around hoping to catch unsuspecting young men to force them into having sex. We imagine that gay men want to have sex with anyone who is male. This isn't true. Just as straight boys are attracted to some girls but not others, gay boys find some — not all — boys attractive. So if you know that someone is gay, you shouldn't feel like you have to avoid going into the boys' toilets with him. Relax; he's not going to try to have sex with you. And remember, if anyone — straight or gay — tries to force you to have sex, you should tell a responsible adult.

  A lot of people also think that all gay men are paedophiles (people who have sex with children). This isn't true either. Yes, there are *some* men out there who like to 'pick up' young boys for sexual activity. But there are many, many more gay men — most, in fact — who aren't interested in that kind of thing at all. The advice to you is still the same; if someone older is hassling you or making you feel uncomfortable, don't hang around with him, and make sure you tell someone. But don't assume that all gay men are chasing young boys, because it simply isn't true.

And being friends with someone who is gay won't turn you gay. Your gay friend isn't trying to recruit you. He probably doesn't even like you in that way.

- **Myth 2:** *You can tell if someone is gay simply by looking at them.* As far as I know, there's no gay mark that all homosexual people have. The fact that someone talks in a high voice, or throws a ball a certain way or likes to knit is not a sign that they are gay. And a goal-scoring record, an interest in motor racing or a full beard in Year 7 does not mean that the person is definitely straight. There are gay men who look big, tough and manly, and straight men who are a little 'effeminate', which means woman-like. So these things are not definite signs.

- **Myth 3:** *You can catch diseases like AIDS from gay people.* This one is actually true, *but* we've talked about how you can catch a whole bunch of diseases from straight people as well. You can get HIV/AIDS, hepatitis and other nasties from having sex with *anyone* who carries those diseases, no matter whether they prefer

BEING FRIENDS WITH SOMEONE WHO IS GAY WON'T TURN YOU GAY

boys or girls. This is why **safe sex** is so important, for straight *and* gay people.

If you were to ask a hundred gay people to name the most difficult thing about being gay, they would almost all say the same thing: that a lot of people don't understand it — or them — at all. And because they don't understand being gay, they're scared of people who are. Fortunately a lot of young people are more accepting now of gay and lesbian people of their own age, which means that **coming out** (telling others about your homosexuality) is a little easier than it used to be. But it can still be a hard thing to do, telling friends and family that you're gay. It takes a lot of bravery.

COMING OUT TAKES A LOT OF BRAVERY

Even if you don't like the idea of what gay people do or how they feel, it is not OK to pick on them, bully them, make fun of them or make them feel bad about being who they are. Everyone has the right to be themselves, and being cruel won't make them change anyway — it will just hurt them.

What if *you're* gay, or think that you might be? Then you should definitely find someone you trust, so that you can talk about your feelings or get support. If you can't discuss it with someone from your family, a friend or a teacher, make an appointment to talk to a doctor or your school counsellor.

And don't be ashamed of who you are, no matter who that person is.

From: Worried

To: richard_the_wise@hotmail.com

Subject: Is my friend gay?

Hi, Richard the Wise, I have a question for you. My best friend has been my mate since we started school, and we've always done loads of stuff together. We play football together, we're on the same teams, and we go to the skate park almost every weekend.

But then the other day we'd been BMXing in the rain and we got all muddy, and before my mum would let us in the house she said we had to have a shower to get the mud off. So I was in the downstairs shower, and just as I was getting out my friend was getting in. And as he handed me a towel I saw that he had an erection. I think he might have been excited because we were in the bathroom together. I kind of ignored it, but then I started to worry about it. What if he was checking me out? I mean, I know I'm not gay, but what if he is? And now he's invited me over to his place to stay this Friday night, and I'm worried that he's going to try to get into bed with me or something.

How do I know if he's gay, and if he is, how do I stop him trying to be gay with me?
Worried

From: richard_the_wise@hotmail.com

To: Worried

Subject: Re: Is my friend gay?

Dear Worried,

Phew, where do I start? OK, just because a boy gets an erection around another boy

doesn't make him gay. It might have been one
of those ones you get at a difficult moment,
or he might have just been thinking about sex
(with someone else, not necessarily you!). If
he'd said, 'Hey, dude, check *this* out. I've got a
chubby. Would you like to touch it? Go on, you'll
like it!' I might be inclined to think he's gay, but
one erection is not a definite sign.

I don't think you should call off the
sleep-over. If he tries to get into bed with you
(which I doubt he's going to do, by the way),
you should just use the method you'd use with
anyone who was doing something you don't feel
comfortable with: tell them that you're unhappy
with what's happening.

If your friend is gay, he needs to know that
you're still going to be his friend. You see,
people who are gay often have to 'come out'.
Coming out can be a difficult thing to do,

so your friend would need to know that you support him. It doesn't mean you have to be his boyfriend —— he might not even like you in that way —— but he needs friends who understand him. He also needs someone who can help him to be strong, because facing ignorant people can be pretty tough. Especially if those ignorant people are supposed to be your friends.

But until you get some kind of clear sign that your friend is gay, I wouldn't worry too much about it. And try not to stare.

Cheers,

RICHARD THE WISE

9 YOUR PENIS: A USER'S MANUAL

All right, I know that your penis doesn't really need a user's manual. I mean, it doesn't even have any moving parts. Right?

Wrong. Your penis is actually a very complicated bit of equipment. It might look like a long, skin-coloured sausage, but what goes on inside your penis is quite interesting.

Most of the time your penis just hangs loose. But when you get excited, or aroused, your brain sends signals to your penis, and little valves in its blood vessels close, trapping blood in special compartments that run along its full length. This is what makes your penis swell in size and become erect. Some erections stick straight out, some point skywards, others are still a little downward-pointing, and some even have a bit of a bend to one side. But one thing is almost always the same: when you get an erection, your penis gets bigger and harder.

When a baby boy is born, his penis has a hood of skin at the end of it. This is called the **foreskin**, and when the penis gets erect, the foreskin pulls back so that the head of the penis is exposed. Parents of some religions like their boys to be **circumcised**, or have their foreskin cut off, but it's not as common as it used to be. With most boys there's no good medical reason to be circumcised, and that's why most baby boys these days get to keep their foreskin.

When you shower or take a bath, you should pull the foreskin back and clean underneath it. If you don't do this, you can get an infection. Just make sure that you roll it back down afterwards, otherwise it can cause problems later.

Even though getting cancer in your testicles is a very small risk at your age, examining your testicles is a good habit to get into. Basically you feel your testicles through the skin of your scrotum. They should both be about the same size, with a small and slightly sensitive bump on the top of each one. If you notice that one testicle is *much* bigger than the other, or if you feel any strange lumps, or if it really hurts to touch either of your testes, you should ask a doctor to check it out.

Penises come in all sizes and shapes. Some hang long, others pull up into themselves. Some are quite small, others are very big. Men sometimes joke about penis size, as if having a big one makes you more of a man. This isn't true. Guys with smaller penises shouldn't worry, since erection seems to even things up quite a bit. Little penises become erect to a particular size, while bigger ones get harder but often don't get a lot bigger.

PENISES COME IN ALL SIZES AND SHAPES

Besides, you shouldn't forget what we talked about earlier: your brain is just as important a sex organ as your penis.

So there you have it. Your penis is a very valuable thing. It's not the only thing that makes you a male, but it's a pretty good place to start, so take care of it. You're never going to get another one.

Once again George had made the mistake of talking before thinking.

Wow - I've seen small ones before but that's just...

tHe 'S' word

From: Thumb, Thomas

To: richard_the_wise@hotmail.com

Subject: Am I normal?

Dear Richard the Wise,

I'm a bit worried that my penis isn't going to get any bigger. All my friends are bigger than they used to be, but mine is still this tiny little thing. When we get changed for sport, they're all walking around with their man-sized penises while I stand in the corner getting changed as fast as I can so no one will see me. I haven't even got pubic hair yet!

What if my incy little penis never grows? Will I be deformed forever?

Tom Thumb

The 'S' word

From: richard_the_wise@hotmail.com

To: Thumb, Thomas

Subject: Re: Am I normal?

Dear Tom Thumb,

Fear not. First, guys develop at different rates. You'll catch up; it might just take a year or two longer.

And even if you did stay small forever, the size of your penis when it's just hanging around doesn't have a lot to do with how big it is when it's erect. In other words, once you get an erection, how small it is at any other time won't matter. You can still enjoy having sex, and so can the girl who has it with you. Size isn't the biggest … sorry, the *main* … thing to worry about anyway. Good sex has more to do with showing someone how you feel about them than some concern about how big your penis is.

But I'm sure it'll be fine. Write to me again in three years if it's still the size of a pinky finger.

Cheers,

RICHARD THE WISE

10 GIRLS, GIRLS, GIRLS

Girls are an odd bunch, really. They're into a lot of stuff that most boys have no interest in. They like fashion, they text and phone and message each other *all* the time, they stick posters of TV stars and bands on their bedroom walls. And that's fine, because the truth is that girls think that the stuff *you're* interested in is a bit weird as well. Motorbikes, wrestling, football, fast cars, computer games — all that stuff is as mysterious to girls as a hot pink, chick-flick and popcorn slumber-party is to you.

Even the ways girls handle their relationships with one another is different. Boys sometimes have a bit of a fight or disagreement, and you might have a sworn rival or enemy, such as the guy who thinks that he should be the team captain when you know that you should be. But most of the time boys deal with their rivalries in a fairly simple way: they either sort it out by fighting or they just ignore each other and get on with life.

Girls are different. Often it's not until the first or second year of secondary school that girls finally settle down into some kind of solid group of friends. And *that* is the group you must break into if you want a particular girl to be your girlfriend.

Having a girlfriend can be a lot of different things. Sometimes a girlfriend is someone you just give that name to, simply because you feel like you need a girlfriend to be more grown up. Often these kinds of girlfriends are handed a note by some in-between person, asking if they want to 'go out' with you. As part of this job, their duties include teasing, chasing and ignoring you, and sometimes being teased, chased and ignored *by* you.

A bit later on you might notice that someone catches your attention. You start thinking about her all the time, and you want to know what she's doing every minute of the day. And the first thing you want to do is

impress her. She needs to notice you, and to notice what a great catch *you* are.

IMPRESSING A GIRL

This desire to impress the female of the species isn't a new thing, and it's not something that just humans do. When a guy shows off, it isn't that different from the mating rituals of birds and animals. You might have seen a peacock strutting about with his feathers all fanned out behind him. There's one reason behind that behaviour — sex. He wants the female — the peahen — to look at him and think, 'Crikey, check out *that* guy! I think I'm going to have to have *sex* with him!' Which eventually leads to peachicks, and the species continues on.

SHOWING OFF ISN'T THAT DIFFERENT FROM THE MATING RITUALS OF BIRDS AND ANIMALS

A boy being cheeky to a teacher, or running screaming across the school yard in pursuit of his screaming best mate, or getting his guitar out at the school bus stop, is just like that peacock. He might not know it, but what he's actually saying is, 'Hey, girls, look at me! I'm the most talented guy around, and if you're looking for a father for your children, I'm your man!' Which is kind of funny, because even though he probably isn't her man at all, he'll still try to prove that he is. And not just to one girl, but to *all* girls.

Men and boys stop showing off to women just before their 130th birthday. Sure, they might get a bit less obvious about it, and they might not even be looking for someone to have their babies, but they still do it. They want women to notice them, and they want to be attractive. And sometimes that desire leads to dangerous and stupid behaviour.

So if you already know that doing a bellyflop off the 10-metre diving board is going to hurt you, maybe even kill you, but not impress a single one of those gorgeous girls looking on, you might be wondering what you *are* supposed to do to impress them. You might ask, 'What if I want a girl-friend? No one's going to notice me if I just do my homework, go to school, behave myself, and play football with the other guys at lunchtime.'

Sure, that might be true, if all girls were the same. But they're not. Some girls are really attracted to boys who are quiet and do their own thing, while others are attracted to boys who chase after them (and I don't mean with a wet tennis

... and conversely, it can be divided by its square root to form a beautiful prime number!

Sam really knew how to charm the girls in advanced maths.

ball!). Certain kinds of people attract certain other kinds of people, and why you find one person more attractive than another is a bit of a mystery. It's been called 'chemistry', and that's about as scientific as this little book gets. It can't really be explained; it just *is*.

It might surprise you to learn that girls are pretty smart. They can tell when a boy is trying to be something that he's not. And that kind of fakeness is a big turn-off to most girls. So the simple solution is to just be yourself.

This is where you might say, 'But when I jump off the bus shelter roof into a pile of rubbish bins I *am* being myself. It's kinda what I *do*!' Yes, that's fair enough, but I'm yet to meet a girl who watches a boy do something stupid and immediately picks up her phone to get his number. She might pick up her phone to call an ambulance, but that's about it.

'All right, then, that's all fine, but there's this one girl that I really like,' you're saying. 'I *really* want to impress her.'

GIRLS CAN TELL WHEN A BOY IS TRYING TO BE SOMETHING THAT HE'S NOT

OK, OK –
I've just got
to be myself...

Of course you do, because you just know that if you don't get to her first, some other guy is going to snap her up (mainly because she feels sorry for him after he broke his collar-bone jumping off the bus shelter roof into a pile of rubbish bins). And you know that if you do get to her too late and you lose her, there'll never be another girl as good, or as perfect for you.

True, there *may* never be another girl as good, but it's also pretty likely that there *will* be. But let's pretend that this *is* the girl for you. You want to impress her. Here then are a few tips for getting the right kind of attention from that perfect girl.

1. **Presentation**. Yes, I know this seems like an obvious one, but before you decide to skip this bit I'm not going to talk about combing your hair or brushing your teeth, although that is actually pretty good advice. (Deodorant goes a long way as well, Stinky. Especially after a sweaty game of lunchtime basketball. But not too much. Moderation is good.)

   No, when I say presentation, I'm talking about how you present yourself to the girl. Are you giving her the best, most appealing you there is? The main two things to think about are smiling and making eye contact. These aren't hard to do, but they can be hard to remember. Let's face it, it can be tricky smiling at a girl when you think that you're about to throw up all over her science project.

But ask most women what attracts them to a man, and they'll usually say a pleasant smile, nice eyes and a good sense of humour. But even if you don't think you've got a pleasant smile or nice eyes, you need to let her see them so she can decide for herself.

Besides, a smile and eye contact tell her that you're confident, and girls really like …

2. **Confidence**. It's true that if you're a shy person you can't just wave a wand and make yourself confident. And don't forget, that quiet nature of yours might be what she really likes about you. But even if you don't *feel* confident, you can still make it look like you are. All it takes is a bit of courage. Conversation openers like 'I think you're cool' or 'Can I be your cooking partner?' aren't the same as asking her to marry you. And seriously, what's the worst that can happen? She can say, 'Well, I don't like *you*', which would be pretty awful but not world-ending, or she could say, 'I've already got a cooking partner'. But at least she knows you're interested. And she knows that you're confident.

So if you want to talk to a girl, calm your

butterflies, walk up to her and say 'Can I sit here?', and if she says 'OK', you're part-way there.

Now all you have to do is …

3. **Listen**. Honestly, girls like guys who listen. That doesn't mean you can't have an opinion or say anything, but just listening will make a girl think that you're the ant's pants. (Actually, now I think about it, it's pretty important that you do in fact say something. If you just sit there silently nodding your head, she's probably going to think you're a bit of a weirdo.)

... and another thing – I'm a really good listener – top shelf! So if you've got something to say – I'm your man – Sam's the man, except my name's not Sam – but you know what I mean don't you … ah, what's your name again?

I'm not suggesting that you *pretend* to listen. If you do that, she'll know. Also, if you're not really listening you won't get to learn all those interesting things that are going on in her head. That's all stuff you want to know about her.

And don't be scared to speak up if you don't agree with something she says; just do it politely. Her opinion might be different from yours, but that doesn't make it wrong. Being able to disagree politely is a sign of …

4. **Respect**. These days we see a lot of disrespect. Many young people don't respect older people, a lot of

older people don't respect the feelings of kids, students don't respect their teachers, and some teachers get annoyed by kids and don't try very hard to hide it.

Passengers on buses and trains don't give up their seats to old people or pregnant women any more, kids and parents don't respect each other, husbands and wives can say really nasty things to each other.

Because of this sad picture, when someone *does* show respect, it really stands out. And if you show a girl respect, she'll almost always respect you in return. That doesn't mean that you have to stand up when she enters the room, or salute, or throw your jumper over a puddle so she can walk across it, but little things like carrying her violin case or opening the door for her tell her a lot more about the kind of boy you are and the kind of man you're becoming than all the showing-offy things you could do in a year of free periods.

HER OPINION MIGHT BE DIFFERENT FROM YOURS, BUT THAT DOESN'T MAKE IT WRONG

From: Eager

To: richard_the_wise@hotmail.com

Subject: How do I get her to notice me?

Dear Richard the Wise,

What are some things I should do to get noticed by this girl I like? I want to impress her, but I don't know how.

Thanks,

Eager

From: richard_the_wise@hotmail.com

To: Eager

Subject: Re: How do I get her to notice me?

Dear Eager,

Rather than listing the things you *should* do, let me list a few things you definitely should *not* do. None of these things will impress her at all. I promise.

1. Being able to belch the national anthem.

2. Being able to fart the national anthem.

3. Being able to belch and fart at the same time, even if it's the national anthem.

4. Being able to recite *pi* to anything more than five decimal places. Same goes for being able to say any of the times tables over twelve.

   Or listing prime numbers. Hello? Boring!

5. Being able to name every Liverpool captain since Emlyn Hughes.

6. Pinching her stuff (and I don't mean her bum, rude boy!). You might think that running off with her diary is hysterical and kind of alluring, but I'm assured by several girls that it's not. Especially if you start reading it aloud to the entire class.

7. Riding your bike down the long flight of steps near the library.

8. Riding *her* bike down the long flight of steps near the library.

9. Setting fire to anything.

10. Pulling your Speedos up the crack of your bum, either because you think it looks funny or because you once saw some surf-lifesavers do it on TV.

11. Wearing Speedos at all, unless you're about to compete in a race. And it should probably be a swimming race.

12. Trying to swim the length of the local pool underwater and almost drowning in the attempt. (Especially if you're wearing Speedos. And even more especially if those Speedos are pulled up the crack of your bum at the time.)

13. Putting anything (e.g. a pencil, a piece of chalk, your finger) up your nose.

14. Participating in eating competitions of any kind: hot-dogs, burgers, pizza, custard. Boogers.

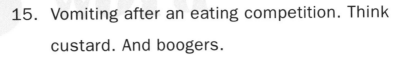

15. Vomiting after an eating competition. Think custard. And boogers.

16. Getting drunk.

17. Getting drunk and vomiting.

18. Smoking.

19. Smoking and vomiting.

20. Smoking, drinking and vomiting.

21. Anything you do immediately after saying, 'Hey, watch this!'

22. Anything you do immediately after saying, 'Guys, you weren't watching! Here, I'll do it again.'

I hope this helps. And if it doesn't help, good luck.

RICHARD THE WISE

dATING

Sometimes when we say *dating* we're talking about two people who are in a special relationship. Other terms we use are 'going out', 'going steady' or 'boyfriend and girlfriend'.

But in this chapter we'll be talking about actually going out *on a date*.

The first and hardest part of going on a date is usually finding the courage to ask a girl whether she'd like to go on a date with you in the first place. Of course, it helps if you have a plan for what you're going to do on this date. If you say, 'Would you like to go out with me some time?', and she says that she would, it would be handy to have a suggestion on hand, rather than just standing there with a stupid look on your face.

The cinema's a great place for a first date. Because you're watching a film, there's less pressure on you to keep the conversation going. And the cinema isn't all that expensive. Also, if you want to be a real gentleman, you can let her choose the film.

THE MOVIES ARE A GREAT PLACE FOR A FIRST DATE

This doesn't mean that you have to go and see the chick-flick about the girl in the iron lung who wants to be a famous ballerina against all the odds, but you should choose to see something you're both happy with. (You might be desperate to see the latest Supercross Devils film, but she probably won't be.) Besides, you can think of it this way: the point of the date isn't about the film you go to see but the fact that you're doing something *together*.

So you've planned the date, you've asked the girl if she'd like to come to the cinema with you, and she's said that she would. Woo-hoo! Well done. The next step is arranging to pick her up, unless she's happy to meet you there. Picking up is probably the best way. It impresses her parents for a start, but it's also just good manners. If the cinema isn't within walking distance of your house you might need to ask one of your parents to give you a lift, but if you plan well enough ahead that shouldn't be too hard to arrange.

I don't care if there is a pony in it – I do not want to see 'Zombie Motocross Killers V'!

Here are a couple of useful tips for your first date.

- **Hygiene**. Have a shower, brush your teeth, put on deodorant and wear clean clothes. (And remember, too much aftershave is worse than none at all.) You don't have to wear a tie or anything silly like that, but something clean and not too old will impress.

- **Be on time**. This can be tricky. Too early and you'll catch her with her hair wrapped in a towel and she'll freak out. Too late and she'll be all worked up by the time you ring the doorbell. And don't forget, she's probably just as nervous as you are, so don't make it harder for her than it needs to be.

- **Talk to her parents**. If her dad opens the door, smile, say hello, even shake his hand. Ask him if his daughter is ready. If he invites you in, accept the invitation. If her mum offers you a drink and you're feeling too sick in the stomach to put anything in it, just say 'No, thank you'. Basically, remember your manners.

DASICALLY, REMEMBER YOUR MANNERS

- **Compliment her**. I don't think people take flowers or chocolate on their first date any more, but one thing that has never gone out of fashion is a good, honest compliment. You don't have to tell her that her eyes are like rock pools that you wish you could dive into, or that she smells as fresh as a summer morning, but saying that she looks nice won't kill you. And she'll like it. She will.

- **Paying for stuff**. Back in the late fifteenth century when your parents were first dating, the man usually paid for everything. These days most girls take money along with them on a date, and are even happy to spend some of it. Still, make sure that you have enough money to pay for everything if you have to. Don't even ask whether she wants you to buy the tickets. Just walk up to the counter and ask for *two* tickets. It looks *very* bad to buy just one ticket then wait for her to buy her own.

After you've bought the tickets she might say, 'I'll get the snacks if you like'. You should probably refuse, but if she really wants to don't make a fuss. It may be that she wants to pay for something so that she feels that the date is a real 'together' thing. But if she doesn't offer, don't worry about it. Just ask her what she'd like, buy the pick'n'mix and popcorn, and enjoy the date.

- **Enjoying the date**. This might seem like an unnecessary thing to say, but don't forget to have fun. It's not very likely that you'll want to hold her hand or kiss her or anything like that on your very first date, but if you do, just make sure that your friends aren't sitting a couple of rows behind you. I think you know why *that* is.

And what should you talk about on the date? Well, it might surprise you to know that girls are just normal people, and they like to talk about the same sort of stuff you do — families, their pets, school, that kind of thing. And remember, any nerves you're feeling, she's probably feeling too. So just chat, and don't worry too much about trying to

It was fully sick n' that - way freaky ! I was like whoa ... heavy dude .

Wicked .

Eventually Ethan and Rachel found they had much in common .

IT MIGHT SURPRISE YOU TO KNOW THAT GIRLS ARE JUST NORMAL PEOPLE

impress her. If you've done everything mentioned so far, she's probably impressed already. But there'll be more talk about conversation in a little while.

- **After the date**. After the date is over and it's time to say goodbye, thank her, and say you'll see her at school or wherever. If you had a really awful time and never want to go out with her again, that's OK, just don't ask her again. But for now, it's polite to thank her for a pleasant date, even if it was less fun than unloading a truckload of marbles with a pitchfork.

There are plenty of other things you can do for a date if going to the cinema isn't your thing:

- **Plan to have lunch together outside of school**. This is a good idea, but be prepared for people to notice. They will, and they'll tell you what you did, as if you didn't already know. 'Hey, you and Samantha had lunch together on Saturday!' Well spotted, Einstein.

- **Ice skating**. Skating isn't too expensive (about the same as the cinema, usually), it's fun, and you don't have to talk the whole time, so there's less pressure. Plus you might have to hang onto each other so you don't fall over. And afterwards you can buy her a drink at the kiosk. A perfect fun date. Just don't let her catch you staring at the slinky staff-member doing pirouettes in her low-cut jeans.

- **Going somewhere like an aquarium or to a football match**. These sorts of dates can cost quite a bit, but they're a lot of fun. Of course, if you decide you'd like to invite her to a football match, you might like to check that she likes football first. And don't wear body paint. Not the first time, anyway.

- **Theme parks**. Warning: this can get *very* expensive. But theme parks are a great place for a date, because they are fun, and there are any number of things to do and talk about. *And* she'll hang onto you tightly on the ghost train.

- **Family events like picnics, barbecues and trips to the beach**. Ask your parents first if it's OK for you to invite someone along, in case they've planned for it to be actual family only. And remember, your nerves will be twice as jangly, knowing that your parents are probably watching you and going, 'Oh, isn't that cute!'

- **A walk in the country or a bike ride**. These are good because you're doing something, and there's not too much pressure to keep the conversation going. And here's a tip: take something nice along for lunch. Surprise her. Girls like picnics. They think they're romantic.

- **A game of tennis**. But if you're a great player and she's never played, don't try to show her how good you are by hitting thirty aces past her, or by making a Slazenger tattoo in the middle of her forehead. But don't pretend that you're hopeless either. And if *she's* a great player and puts thirty aces past *you*, don't throw stuff or stomp off home. Girls hate that. Just remember to have fun.

- **The school dance**. The only problem with this one is that your friends will probably be there, and since they're such total losers they won't have a girl to take along. This means that they'll spend the whole night sitting in a group chortling at you. But that's cool, because you're the one with the cute girl.

From: Desperate

To: richard_the_wise@hotmail.com

Subject: Wicked girl alert!

Hi, Richard the Wise,

There's this girl at school, and she's wicked.

(When I say she's wicked, I mean that she's

really nice.) I want to ask her if she'll go out with me, but I don't know how. I'm not sure, but the whole 'Do you like me? Tick yes or no' letter seems a bit babyish. Help!

Desperate

From: richard_the_wise@hotmail.com

To: Desperate

Subject: Re: Wicked girl alert!

Dear Desperate,

When you say you want this nameless girl to 'go out' with you, do you mean actually go to the cinema or something like that, or do you mean that you want to ask her to be your girlfriend? Because these things have a natural kind of order of progression. But it's a little complicated, so I'll break it down into steps. Are you ready?

1. Talk to the girl. A lot.
2. Repeat step 1.

3. Ask her if she'd like to go on a date with you. To the cinema, or for a drink at a café, Chinese burns in the library, something like that. Definitely not going with you and your mates to watch the wrestling.

4. Repeat step 1. And step 2. And step 3 as well.

5. Go back to step 4.

That's it. Do that for a while and one of two things will happen. You'll either have a girlfriend that you've done heaps of fun stuff with, or you'll realise that this groovy chick you thought was going to be an awesome girlfriend is actually not your type at all. Or she might decide the same

thing about you, all on her own. Which would be awful, but that's life.

So don't just march up to some girl you hardly know and say, 'You're cute. Do you want to be my girlfriend?' Because even if she says 'Yes', she won't be your girlfriend. She'll just be a girl you hardly know who claims that you're her boyfriend. Good luck.

RICHARD THE WISE

PS: One more tip. Girls are not impressed by a boy who freely demonstrates that he can drink Coke through his nose.

From: Tongue-tied

To: richard_the_wise@hotmail.com

Subject: Please help!

Dear Richard the Wise,

I'm about to go on a date with a girl, and I'm really worried that we'll run out of things to talk about. I don't want her to think that I'm boring, but I'm quite shy. What if the conversation totally dries up?

Do you have any suggestions?

Tongue-tied

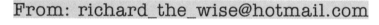

From: richard_the_wise@hotmail.com

To: Tongue-tied

Subject: Re: Please help!

Dear Tongue-tied,

First, congratulations on getting a girl to go out with you. If you're really that shy, it must have been hard finding the courage to invite her to begin with. You rock!

Stuff to talk about, huh? OK, try these, because once you get started you're away.

- Ask about her family or her pet. If she says, 'I've got a dog', ask her what the dog's name is. Ask her stuff. And listen to the answers. Then ask another question. Maybe say what you think about what she just said, then ask her another question. Then listen some more. And a bit more.

- What's her favourite subject at school, and why? What's yours, and why? The thing is, you're looking for conversation, not just you going, 'What's your favourite food?', 'What's your favourite colour?', 'Have you tried a tomato sauce smoothie?', like you're interviewing her for a job. So when she tells you that her favourite subject is history because she likes seeing how and why things happened in the past, that's when *you* reply, 'I like history too, but I think I like maths better. At least with maths you know that there's only one right answer.'

- This question is always good for a conversation starter: 'If you were going to be stuck on a desert island for a long time and you could take one book, one movie and one CD, what would they be?' (Of course, if she says *Saddle Club*, *Princess Diaries* and a

CD by some rather pathetic boy band, try to resist the urge to stick your finger down your throat like you're going to spew. Nod, smile, say something neutral like, 'Really? Which track is your favourite? Because I think number two is OK.'

- If you talk about death, she might think you're a bit creepy. But if you are feeling brave, ask her what her final meal would be. (Mine would be an Indian banquet. One that never ends. And I'd eat *very* slowly.)

- Oh, this is a good one! I just thought of it! Ask her what she wants to do when she grows up. But if she says something odd, like a blubber analyst for the department of fisheries, replying, 'Are you *serious*?' might kill the mood. Nod, smile again, and come back with, 'Blubber, huh? I don't know much about blubber.'

- Don't make stuff up. If you tell her stuff that isn't quite true, you're going to find it hard to remember what you've said and what you haven't. I mean it, dude. Even if you are quite boring, I think she'd rather that than someone who claims he's got a black belt in karate but then gets his lunch money pinched by the First Year bully. That's just embarrassing.

So keep it simple and real.

The main thing to remember is this: once you get into a proper conversation and actually start talking and listening to each other, you tend to forget that you're on a date and that you're meant to be having a conversation. Because you actually are, and keeping a real conversation going is much easier than trying to think of a way to start a new one.

Oh, and there's one more thing. Palm cards or notebooks filled with lists of questions are

not cool. *Not* cool. Neither is having a friend in a van outside feeding clever lines into your earpiece. This might work in the movies, but it would be a pretty stupid girl who didn't notice the cable coming out of your ear.

Be brave, and have fun.

RICHARD THE WISE

HAVING A GIRLFRIEND

Having a girlfriend is a tricky business. For a start, this might feel like the 'real thing' to you, especially after you've gone on a couple of dates and you've asked her if she wants to be your girlfriend. But while you're thinking that this is really great and might even be the 'real thing', it could be difficult to get your parents or other grown-ups or even some of your friends to take it seriously.

Some of the things that impress girls were listed earlier, and these things keep impressing girlfriends as well. Respect, confidence and courtesy are all very important when you have a girlfriend. Sometimes she might want to hang with her friends at lunchtime, or you might want to go to the skatepark with your mates after school, and respect means that you let each other do those sorts of things. Having a girlfriend doesn't mean that you can't do anything without her. Sometimes you will have to let her go and do stuff by herself or with her friends, and she will do the same for you.

But a lot of the time you'll want to do things together. This is what it really means to have a girl-friend — wanting to share experiences. And having a girlfriend when you're young is good practice for when you're older, because many of the problems that adults have with their partners are a lot like the ones you might face with your first girlfriend: problems like jealousy, finding time for each other, and communication misun-derstandings.

Communication is the biggest one of the lot. We hear people talking about this all the time, but that's only because it's true. And this goes for boys who are in relationships with other boys as well. Any close rela-tionship between two people, whether they're gay or straight, needs the communication to be strong, because if it isn't misunderstandings can arise, and it all starts to get messy and selfish.

It's very easy to forget about communicating with someone we're close to. This sounds weird, I know, but when someone is your partner, you feel sure that they're always going to be there. And because of that, you stop talking to them. You don't feel like you have to impress them any more, so you stop trying, and eventually things start to get a bit creaky. Add a bit of jealousy and suddenly you've got a relationship that isn't working very well.

So the secret to a good relationship isn't that much of a secret. If something is worrying you, discuss it. If something your girlfriend has said makes you cross, tell her. If something makes you happy, talk about it. Ask her what she thinks. This girlfriend of yours is supposed to be just that — a girl*friend*. So talk to her like a friend. In other words, be open about your feelings rather than bottling them up like many men seem to do. Don't be frightened to tell her that you feel down, happy, confused or angry. She'll respect you for it, and it will help you understand your own feelings. Plus it's good practice for when you're an adult. In a world of men who are scared to express themselves, you'll stand out. And you'll stand out in a good way.

ANY CLOSE RELATIONSHIP NEEDS THE COMMUNICATION TO BE STRONG

If you communicate well, one of the other big problems you might face becomes less of a problem — jealousy and lack of trust. If you can talk about how you feel, and if she feels that she can as well, you're going to trust each other a lot more. And that's really what a good relationship is all about.

Hey, Richard the Wise,

I want to kiss my girlfriend. I've managed to kiss her on the cheek, and she seemed to like that. She actually kissed me back, which was cool. But now I want to know how to kiss her properly. I've been practising, but the mirror is so cold, and it doesn't kiss back.

Smoochy

From: richard_the_wise@hotmail.com

To: Smoochy

Subject: Re: Help required

Dear Smoochy,

First, forget everything you've seen in films. I say that even though I don't know what films you've seen. But most of them will be wrong, especially for the first time you kiss a girl.

First, there'll be no music building and swelling behind you. So as far as a soundtrack goes, you're pretty much on your own. Second, in the movies, soon after the kissing starts the director often fades out and cuts to the next scene, where the happy couple are sitting on the balcony in their bathrobes sipping tea or cuddling in front of the fire. Or sometimes they're in bed, but you shouldn't be going *there* after your first kiss. But what the movies don't show is the uncomfortable moment after the kiss ends, when you find yourself clearing your throat and looking for a reason to leave the room. What I'm saying is: don't kiss in such a way that you have to feel embarrassed.

So, how is that? The answer is: take your time. Start slowly. Don't ram your tongue down her throat the moment your lips meet. Kiss her like you're kissing eggshells, softly and gently. Treat her mouth like the most delicious ice-cream cone you've ever had, rather than like a Big Mac that you just devour. There's time for all the tongue-hockey later on, but for now make it slow and gentle. If you do that, you won't need a soundtrack, and you'll be glad there's no fadeout.

Enjoy.

RICHARD THE WISE

GIRLS ARE DIFFERENT

Generally speaking, girls look at the world differently. They can be hard — even impossible — to understand. They can change their mind about something in a split second. One minute they think one thing, and the next they'll be thinking the exact opposite. And are you cool with that? Well, guess what, you have to be.

Why are girls the way they are? A lot of it has to do with hormones, which are the chemicals in our body that affect things like how and when we develop, the things that make us feel attracted to someone, and what makes us get sexually excited. When girls reach puberty, their hormones can make their moods go a bit wobbly. They can fly into a storm of tears or a fit of anger without too much warning, and afterwards wonder what the people around them are so upset about. But they're not putting it on; sometimes they honestly can't see what all the fuss is about.

This doesn't stop when a young woman is fully developed, although it can be a lot worse during puberty. An earlier chapter discussed how a woman releases an egg every twenty-eight days or so, and if the egg isn't fertilised the woman menstruates, or has a period. Well, it's hormones that make all that happen, and those same hormones can affect her moods, especially in the days just before her period starts. This is why about once a month or so your mum or your older sister can get really crabby and maybe a bit unreasonable for a day or two. There's a name for this — **premenstrual tension** (PMT) or **premenstrual stress** (PMS). But a word of advice: if your mum, sister or girlfriend get angry with you about something, think hard before you ask them if they're having their period. I can guarantee that a question like that will *not* improve their mood.

Besides, if they're angry with you, there is a remote possibility that you've actually done something really dumb or insensitive, like forgetting their birthday or your one-month anniversary. So before you say 'Have you got PMT?' you might want to check your calendar. It could save your life.

Another thing about girls is that they do care about things that you might not care so much about, like celebrating your first week together. Do it. Buy her a flower or a card. Write her a note saying how much you've enjoyed your first seven days together. You might feel a bit silly, but she'll appreciate it. Thinking about what *she* likes will make the relationship run a lot more smoothly. And guess what? She'll think about what you like as well. It's how it works.

As this book has pointed out several times now, girls often have different interests from boys. They might not understand why you think that watching sport or playing a computer game is more important than talking about something their best friend said to them yesterday. They might not get why that film you love is so good. Girls see a toddler or a cute baby and go all gooey and start acting like they're little mothers, while to you the same baby is just plain noisy, smelly and annoying. That joke you heard and just *had* to tell to the class made you and your friends totally crack up, but all the girls rolled their eyes and acted like your great-aunt Maude: 'That is *so* immature.'

BEFORE YOU SAY 'HAVE YOU GOT PMT?' YOU MIGHT WANT TO CHECK YOUR CALENDAR. IT COULD SAVE YOUR LIFE

Yes, maybe they're right. Maybe it is immature. Or maybe it's just another way that girls are different from boys. But getting on with girls isn't just about putting up with their weird differences. Some of those differences are what makes them so wonderful, and I'm not just talking about their soft skin and curviness. Much of a girl's view of the world comes from the way she's been raised, and a big part of that is the fact that she's female. And those views might sometimes seem a little odd or even crazy to you as a guy, but she's just being who she is. And it's always better when friends are honest about who they are.

So accept who she is, just as you want her to accept who *you* are, and enjoy it.

BREAKING UP

I can hear what you're thinking. 'What? Breaking up? One minute he's talking about going on the first date and communicating, and now he's talking about breaking up? Already? How come?'

Let's imagine for a moment that you have a girlfriend. She's beautiful, she really likes you, maybe you've kissed a couple of times, and you might even have told her that you love her. (Girls like it when you do that, but they can tell if you're lying, so only say it if you really mean it.)

You and your girlfriend are really happy together. You understand that she sometimes wants to hang out with her friends talking about girl stuff, and she's totally fine with you playing football at lunchtime rather than sitting with her. You talk about all kinds of stuff all the time, you trust each other, and you've never once asked her if she's hormonal.

This sounds perfect, doesn't it? It sounds like this relationship is going to last forever. And it might.

Or it might not. It's pretty unusual that people who go out together in school end up together as grown-ups. It does sometimes happen, but not very often. At your age you're both changing very fast, and the stage you're at might not be the same as hers. So there's a good chance that you'll find that you're no longer quite as good for each other as you once were, or once thought you were. You might find that the things that attracted you to each other in the first place don't seem all that important any more. Maybe all you've really got in common is that you both play tennis, and that when you spend time together you've got nothing to talk about except tennis. Maybe you got together with her because she was the coolest girl in the class, and you just happened to be the first boy to find the courage to ask her out. And now, six weeks later … nothing. Or perhaps you both just chose poorly. It happens.

There are many reasons that relationships fail. But the uncomfortable truth is that at some point you're probably going to break up with someone, or someone's going to break up with you.

Breaking up is horrible. It's *always* horrible. If a girl that you really like suddenly decides that she doesn't want to be your girlfriend any more, it hurts. A lot. It feels so bad because what the girl is really saying to you is, 'I don't think that you're as good a person as I thought you were. I think I might have made a huge mistake. You're not the best person for me.' And being rejected like that is very painful.

UNFORTUNATELY, BREAKING UP DOES HAPPEN

Being the person who does the breaking up isn't easy, either. Even if you don't love her, it still feels cruel to say to someone, 'I'm sorry, but I don't want to be your boyfriend any more.' Because that means that you're rejecting *her*. And she's probably going to start crying and run off to her friends. Then she's going to tell them all what a mean and horrible person you are, even if you're really not.

Then maybe you'll have to see each other in class, which is uncomfortable. There'll be glares and stares, and you might hear her crying quietly at the back of the classroom, or see her crying in the playground, and if you ask her if she's OK she'll tell you to get lost. Yes, it gets very messy.

Pretty much everyone breaks up with someone at some time. It's never easy. Even if she's done something terrible that has hurt you more than you ever thought possible, breaking up isn't nice. Being angry doesn't help, so here are some ways that you can cope better with the break-up.

- **Do it face-to-face**. Breaking up over the phone, by note or by friend might seem like the easiest way, but it's not the right way. She'll feel that you're not only rejecting her but that you don't care enough about her to even tell her to her face. So you should be a man, sit down with her and be honest. 'I've been thinking about our relationship. I don't think it's working out. We're only young, and I don't want to be tied down to one person at our age. I really like you, and I've enjoyed being your boyfriend, but I think that our relationship is a bit closer than it should be right now.' Or something like that. It's not going to be easy, but at least it will be said. And you can feel proud that you've faced up to the decision you've made.

- **Don't go back ... yet**. She's definitely going to cry. You know that, right? Accept it. It happens.

I think we're breaking up.

How do you know?!

She hasn't texted me since this morning.

And that's going to make you feel guilty and mean. But if it's a decision that you've thought hard about, don't change your mind the minute her chin starts wobbling. I'm not saying that you shouldn't ever get back with her — lots of people think it over and realise that what they had was really great — but give it a bit of time to get over how awful the break-up feels. Then you'll be able to think more clearly about what happens next.

And what will happen next? Well, once it's all calmed down you might be able to talk about what it was that went wrong. You might have to tell her that she needs to give you more space. She might say that she'd like you to not make fun of her brother's sticky-out ears or pick your nose. But that's all stuff that, once you sort it out, might make the relationship work again. Or not. But at least wait a little while, so the raw emotion of breaking up isn't getting in the way of you thinking straight.

- **What if *she* breaks up with *you*?** Ouch, but try not to get angry. You might feel that way, but try to show her respect. It probably wasn't easy for her to break the bad news to you, so don't make things worse by smashing a window or tattooing 'I hate Jenny' on the back of your knuckles with a drawing pin. Also, you're going to find it almost impossible to think about anything else for a while, and it's going to make you feel miserable. You'll probably even cry a bit, and that's fine. But you *will* get over it. Trust me, you will.

All of this goes for people in same-sex relationships as well. If a break-up happens, be honest, be strong, and be prepared for it to hurt. It's never easy, but it happens.

From: Sleepless

To: richard_the_wise @hotmail.com

Subject: I think I'm in love

Dear Richard the Wise,
There's this girl who I just can't stop thinking about. She's really good-looking, but that's not really why I like her. I like her because I think that

I think we should just stay friends.

I didn't know we were going out!

we're meant to be together. She catches the same bus as me (she goes to the secondary school I'll be going to next year) and she sat next to me the other day. She asked me about my new phone, and we talked for a while, and I think we really hit it off well. I say hi to her most mornings and she talks to me a bit, when she's not with her friends or talking on her phone. And now I can't think about anyone else. I think I'm in love. What should I do?

Sleepless in Sylvania

From: richard_the_wise@hotmail.com

To: Sleepless

Subject: Re: I think I'm in love

Dear Sleepless, Oh yes, I've seen this before. Young love, it's wonderful. I reckon I can tell you what else has been going on. Should I try?

This girl —— let's call her Abby —— has a strange effect on you. Your words, which normally come out so smoothly, suddenly become a series of grunts and mutterings and coughs when you're around her. When you see her coming along the aisle of the bus you catch your breath. And when you think about her, you get this weird feeling in your chest.

You know her phone number, her address, the name of her pet and the names of all her friends. She's got a boyfriend but she complains about him a bit, so she's probably going to dump him real soon and you can be together then. You even feel envious of her possessions because they get to be near her more than you do. You see her in a shop and wish that you had some excuse to be in there as well. Then you *make* an excuse; you go 'looking' for someone just so you can go in there. 'Oh, hi! Have you seen my friend Andrew?' you ask, to which Abby replies, 'Who's Andrew?' And you feel stupid.

You think about her constantly. Her face is the last thing you see when you go to sleep and the first thing you see when you wake up. You write her first name and your last name together, just to see how her full name will look when she marries you. You google her name just in case she's already famous for something and you didn't know. And rather than asking her if she's going to the school disco so you can be sure to see her there, you just hope she will be, and feel dismal and tragic when she's not.

It sounds quite a lot like love, doesn't it?

Well, I've got news for you, bucko. It probably isn't. What I've described is a nasty business called infatuation, which is a kind of unreasonable affection that you develop for someone. Yup, what you've got there is an A-grade crush. The only men who've never had a crush are the ones who were never boys. And a lot of men have crushes even after they stop being boys. Which makes them behave like boys. Get what I'm saying?

My advice? Be friendly, chat with the girl, even be her friend. But, dude, seriously, is a high school girl going to go out with a primary school guy?

RICHARD THE WISE

11 IMAGE, AND BEING A MAN

We're all different shapes and sizes. You'll have noticed that, I'm sure.

But even though we all know this, it seems that no one is completely happy with the way they look. People who are a bit skinny think that they're scrawny. If you're carrying a few too many kilos, you think that you're fat. You wish you had curly hair, straight hair, a smaller nose, bigger eyes, a six-pack, less bendy legs, less sticky-out ears, and the list goes on and on and on. Sometimes we think that it's only girls who worry about that stuff, but guys do as well. And because we think that we aren't good-looking enough, we try to make up for it by showing off or buying the latest cool gadget.

This gets extra tricky around puberty, mostly because people develop at different rates. I remember when I was at school there was one boy in Second Year who had a beard the size of a small sheep, while there were others who hadn't even started shaving off their face-fuzz in Fourth Year. So it can be really hard to work out if you're normal or not when you look around and see how other boys your age are developing.

I don't know what to tell you about this problem. We all have something about ourselves that we'd change if we could, but except for a couple of things — losing or gaining a bit of weight, getting braces for crooked teeth or getting a new haircut — there's not much we can do about it. So we have to work out how to deal with who we are and the body we've been given.

Sometimes we think that we can change who we are by buying new clothes or buying the latest electronic gizmo. These things might change how some people see us, and they might even change how we see ourselves. But they don't change who we really are.

And I've got some more bad news for you. This situation doesn't improve

You're a selfish, bad skinned, socially inept, emotionally retarded young man. In other words — normal!

much as you get older. It's just the price tags on those toys, gadgets and clothes that change. The newest car, boat, house or leather jacket might impress a few people, but in the end those things won't change who you are or what kind of a man you've become.

So, what do you think it is to be a man? Is it having a penis? Is it being able to work hard and earn money for your family? Is it about having a wife or a girlfriend? Is it about being a dad? Is it about having a big, fast car, or being able to score a goal to win a game? Or is it about being able to stand up to some loser down at the pub after he says something rude about your girlfriend?

Being a man is not really about any of those things. They all contribute to who you are as a man, but taking away any of them won't make you less of a man.

Thirty or forty years ago most men went to work and earned money for their families, while their wives stayed at home, raised the kids, cleaned the house and cooked the dinner. It's still this way in some families, but there are also a lot of women now who go to work outside of the home. Women now know that there aren't that many jobs that only men can do. That's why

WE ALL HAVE SOMETHING ABOUT OURSELVES THAT WE'D CHANGE IF WE COULD we have women who are lawyers, doctors, dentists, politicians, architects, truck drivers and so on. Not so long ago these jobs were almost always done by men. Now things have changed.

There are also many more men now who stay at home with the children, or who do a lot more around the house. Many men still think that work like that is only for women, but fortunately there are many who don't.

But this kind of complicates things a bit. Before these changes happened, it was easy to say what it was that made someone a man. He did a manly job, and he had a wife who did the womanly work. Easy. He'd go to the pub for a drink with his mates after work, then come home, put his feet up, and maybe mow the lawn on the weekend. For a lot of guys it's all quite different now.

WHAT IS IT THAT'S GOING TO MAKE YOU A MAN?

So what is it that's going to make *you* a man? And more importantly, what is it that's going to make you a *good* man?

The English writer Samuel Johnson once said, 'The true measure of a man is how he treats someone who can do him absolutely no good' — in other words, being good and not expecting anything in return. And Booker T. Washington, who for the first few years of his life was an African-American slave, said, 'Character, not circumstances, makes the man.'

Bugger! That's a good likeness.

What these wise people were saying was that a true man is someone who can be kind and respectful, and knows he's being as honest and trust-worthy as he can be. And if you can try to be like that in your own life, you'll find that most things go well. You'll be a better lover and partner, a better dad, a better worker and a better friend. Basically, you'll be a better man.

You might find this hard to believe at your age, but one day you'll be old. And one day you'll die, because in the end everyone dies. But when they talk about you after you're gone, no one is going to care about the kind of car you drove or how many goals you kicked, or how old you were when you first had a shave or kissed a girl, or even whether you had muscly arms and a six-pack. They'll be talking about the kind of man

AFTER YOU'RE GONE, NO ONE IS GOING TO CARE ABOUT THE KIND OF CAR YOU DROVE you were, and whether you cared about other people. You'll want them to talk about how kind, respectful, generous and honest you were, and how much you loved your partner and your children, your pets and your friends.

And that's way more important than some big, fast car.

12 FINALLY...

Life is a complicated business. Being a kid is tricky and being an adult is even trickier, but getting safely from boyhood to manhood might be about the trickiest thing there is. Your body is changing, and your parents, teachers, friends and family expect things from you that you might think are stupid or unfair. And worst of all, you're trying to get girls to like you while you attempt to conceal an erection the size of a bowling-pin.

So how can I encourage you? Remember, everyone goes through it. Next time you're in class, look around at the other

Unexpectedly at breakfast, Travis decided to accept his youthful disposition once and for all.

I've got an erection and I feel great!

boys. They're all going through an experience a lot like yours. And they'll get through it, just as you will, even with those annoying erections.

Sometimes it might all feel a bit overwhelming. The good news is that you don't have to battle through it alone. There are people you can talk to, and they can help you. Teachers, parents, friends, school counsellors and older brothers understand what it feels like. You can make an appointment to see a doctor, and *anything* you say to them is totally private.

YOU'RE UNIQUE ... NO ONE ELSE IS EXACTLY LIKE YOU

You're unique, which means that no one else is exactly like you. Yes, I know, you've heard it all before, but it's true. Not one of the six billion other people in the world has exactly the same blend of characteristics as you do. No one else has the same talents or sense of humour as you do. No one has grown up experiencing the world in exactly the same way as you have. So you shouldn't try to be everyone else or anyone else — just be who you are. And if your main objective is to find a girl who likes you, you can take it from me: girls like honesty, and they like boys who are genuine. They like boys who know who they are, and who aren't scared to show it.

Finally, *write it down*. Have a journal. It doesn't have to be anything fancier than an exercise book in your bottom drawer, but make sure that you write on the front that it's private. Then get writing. If something worries you, or makes you happy, or makes you angry, *write it down*. If something confuses you, or you don't know what to do next, *write it down*. And do it every day.

There are two good reasons to do this. First, the act of writing it down helps you think things through and makes those things clearer in your own mind. It also gives you something to look back on later. You'll read over it in two or three years and say, 'I did it. I came through all that weird puberty thing, and I'm OK.' Which will give you so much confidence in the latest and newest issues in your life.

But best of all, in years from now, when your own son is about to go through puberty and he says to you, 'Dad, you don't understand', you can take out your journal, show it to him, and say, 'No, I *do* understand. Let me prove it to you.'

NOTES

NOTES

Notes

NOTES

NOTES

Notes

Notes

NOTES